Photoshop Most Wanted 2:
More Effects and Design Tips

Colin Smith
Al Ward

friendsof

DESIGNER TO DESIGNER™

an Apress® company

Photoshop Most Wanted 2: More Effects and Design Tips

Copyright © 2003 by Colin Smith and Al Ward

ISBN (pbk): 1-59059- 262-X

Printed and bound in the United States of America 10987654321

Trademarked names may appear in this book. Rather than use a trademark symbol with every occurrence of a trademarked name, we use the names only in an editorial fashion and to the benefit of the trademark owner, with no intention of infringement of the trademark.

Distributed to the book trade in the United States by Springer-Verlag New York, Inc., 175 Fifth Avenue, New York, NY, 10010 and outside the United States by Springer-Verlag GmbH & Co. KG, Tiergartenstr. 17, 69112 Heidelberg, Germany.

In the United States: phone 1-800-SPRINGER, email orders@springer-ny.com, or visit http://www.springer-ny.com. Outside the United States: fax +49 6221 345229, email orders@springer.de, or visit http://www.springer.de.

For information on translations, please contact Apress directly at 2560 Ninth Street, Suite 219, Berkeley, CA 94710. Phone 510-549-5930, fax 510-549-5939, email info@apress.com, or visit http://www.apress.com.

The information in this book is distributed on an "as is" basis, without warranty. Although every precaution has been taken in the preparation of this work, neither the author(s) nor Apress shall have any liability to any person or entity with respect to any loss or damage caused or alleged to be caused directly or indirectly by the information contained in this work.

Photoshop Most Wanted 2: More Effects and Design Tips

Credits

Colin Smith is an award winning Graphic Designer who has caused a stir in the design community with his stunning photorealistic illustrations composed entirely in Photoshop. He is also founder of the popular PhotoshopCafe web resource for Photoshop users and web designers. He has won numerous design contests and awards, including Guru Awards at the 2001 Photoshop World Convention in LA, 2002 in San Diego and MacWorld 2002 in NY. Colin's work has been recognized by Photoshop User, Mac Design, Dynamic Graphics, Computer Arts, Studio Multimedia and WWW Internet Life magazines. Colin is also a regular columnist for the NAPP members' site and Planet Photoshop. Between freelance design and writing for foED, he keeps pretty busy. Colin has co-authored New Masters of Photoshop, Foundation Photoshop, Photoshop Most Wanted, Photoshop 7 Trade Secrets, and From Photoshop to Dreamweaver. To Jason Cook, my Dreamweaver teacher, thanks for all the extra help on Ultradev. Thanks Mum for all your encouragement over the years and supporting my dreams, no matter where they have led me. Thanks to Al Ward my co-author, you're a great guy to work with (keep that liquify tool away from me!) Also thanks to your family for the hospitality up there in "big sky" country. To the crew at friends of ED, who never sleep especially Luke and Chris, you guys are great. Thanks to Scott, Jeff, Stacy, Tommy and all my friends at NAPP. To my friends and moderators at the CAFE, especially Frank, Mike, Christian and Realist, you guys make it possible. Finally, thanks to God for supplying the gift and the inspiration.

Al Ward, a certified Photoshop Addict and Webmaster of Action FX Photoshop Resources (www.actionfx.com) hails from Missoula, Montana. A former submariner in the U.S. Navy, Al now spends his time writing on graphics related topics and creating add-on software for Adobe Photoshop and Adobe Elements. Al is the Co-Author (with Colin Smith) of 'Photoshop Most Wanted: Effects and Design Tips', a manual of popular Photoshop Special Effects, and 'Foundation Photoshop 6.0' from Friends of ED Publishing. Al is the Author of Adobe Elements 2 Special Effects, a new solo title from Hungry Minds/Wiley Publishing. He has been a contributor to Photoshop User Magazine, a contributing writer for 'Photoshop Elements 2 – 50 Ways to Create Cool Pictures', 'Photoshop 7 Effects Magic', 'Inside Photoshop 6' and 'Special Edition Inside Photoshop 6' from New Riders Publishing, and writes for several Photoshop related websites including the National Association of Photoshop Professional's Official Website, Photoshop User.Com (http://www.photoshopuser.com), Planet Photoshop (http://www.planetphotoshop.com) and the Photoshop Café (http://www.photoshopcafe.com). Al was a panelist at the Photoshop World 2001 Los Angeles Conference, and contributes to the official NAPP website as the Actions area coordinator. Al lists Scott Kelby, Editor-In-Chief of Photoshop User Magazine as his hero, coffee as his favorite food group, and sleep as the one pastime he'd like to take up some day. In his off time he enjoys his church, his family, fishing the great Northwestern United States and scouring the Web for Photoshop related topics.

Welcome

Back by popular demand, Colin Smith and Al Ward unveil another feast of Photoshop delights.

After the first *Photoshop Most Wanted* book we were deluged with feedback from readers wanting more: more effects so realistic you can almost touch them, more insider knowledge on using Actions and Layer Styles, and more of the inventive designs that have made Al and Colin such respected members of the Photoshop community.

So this is it: a book jam-packed with great effects and cool design tips. You'll learn how to create a whole range of textures from industrial metal to the natural world, you'll discover how to use Masks, Gradients and Filters, and you'll be inspired by the amazing text effects.

The book looks at some of Photoshop most sophisticated effects including how to make authentic-looking 3D objects, as well as examining one of Photoshop's hidden gems – the 3D engine.

We'll also look at the best ways to use Photoshop for the Web, and clever transparency effects. We end the book with two collaborative design projects. We had a lot of positive feedback about the design projects in the first Most Wanted book, and this time Colin boarded planes and flew to Montana to work with Al on some more groundbreaking designs.

As an added extra this book comes complete with a CD, on which you'll find a wealth of goodies, including source files, Actions and Layer Styles from Al, video tutorials from Colin, as well as some exciting bonus tutorials. So, take the book in hand, boot up your computer and prepare for some Photoshop fun!

Conventions

We've tried to keep this book as clear and easy to follow as possible, so we've only used a few layout styles:

- When you come across an important word or phrase, it will be in **bold** type.

- We'll use a different font to emphasize phrases that appear on the 'screen,' `code`, `filenames`, what to hit on the KEYBOARD, and hyperlinks (www.friendsofed.com)

- Menu commands are written in the form Menu > Sub-menu > Sub-menu.

- When there's some information we think is really important, we'll highlight it like this:

> *This is very important stuff – make sure you're paying attention!*

Support – we're here to help

All books from friends of ED aim to be easy to follow and error-free. However, if you do run into problems, don't hesitate to get in touch – our support is fast, friendly, and free.

You can reach us at support@friendsofed.com, quoting the last four digits of the ISBN in the subject of the e-mail (that's 262X in case you're wondering). If you're having technical problems with a specific file that you've created from an exercise, it can sometimes help to include a copy of that file with your mail.

Even if our dedicated support team is unable to solve your problem immediately, your queries will be passed onto the editors and authors to solve.

We'd love to hear from you, whether it's to request future books, ask about friends of ED, or tell us about the images you went on to create after you read this book.

> *To tell us a bit about yourself and make comments about the book, send us an email at* feedback@friendsofed.com

If your enquiry concerns an issue not directly related to any book content, then the best place for these types of questions is our message board lists at:

http://friendsofed.infopop.net/2/OpenTopic

Here, you'll find a variety of designers talking about what they do, who should be able to provide some ideas and solutions.

Chapter 1

Metalworking

Generating metal effects in Photoshop has always been very high on the cool list and remains one of the most popular requests that I receive. In truth there are infinite variations of metal that could be covered.

For this chapter I've chosen my favorite metal effects, and later in the book you'll see Colin unveil his own personal preferences – if you're familiar with the format, then you know that's part of the premise of the Photoshop Most Wanted titles: two designers approaching design from their separate points of view, and meeting somewhere in the middle.

Another note before I begin. In one of these metal tutorials, I use type-shaped objects. The process for achieving these effects can be applied to objects other than type, so don't focus solely on the shape to which the effect is applied, but rather the process used in achieving the effect. This approach should be followed throughout the book. You're not trying to duplicate every nuance in the examples presented, but to learn how to achieve the effect in your own designs.

That being said, let's apply logs to the hearth, fire up the forge, and melt some ore!

1: Silver and gold

1. Open `Background-1.jpg` from the CD source files for this chapter.

2. In the Layers palette, click the 'Create a new layer' icon at the bottom of the palette.

3. Select the Shape tool. In the options bar select Fill Pixels, Custom Shape tool, Normal mode, 100% opacity and Anti-aliased.

4. For this tutorial, I've created a predefined shape using a large font. It's saved with the CD source files for this chapter as `PMW-Chapter 1 Shape.csh`. Load the shape into Photoshop by clicking the menu arrow on the right of the Shape panel in the options bar.

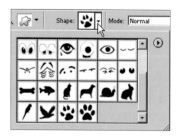

5. When the Shape picker appears, click the arrow in the top right to bring up the Shape menu. Choose Load Shapes… and when the Load dialog appears, browse to `PMW-Chapter 1 Shape.csh` and open it.

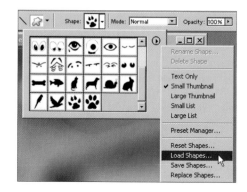

6. The shape now resides in the Shape Picker. Select it.

7. Draw the selected shape on the new layer. Use a dark gray or something in the middle of the gray spectrum.

8. Rename the layer 'chrome-1'. Click the small eye next to the Background layer in the Layers palette to make it invisible.

9. Open the Channels palette. Duplicate the Blue channel by click-dragging the channel to the 'Create new channel' icon at the bottom of the palette. Rename the duplicate channel 'Chrome-1'.

10. Duplicate the Chrome-1 channel. Rename the duplicate 'Chrome-2'. Ensure that Chrome-2 is the only channel with visibility turned on.

11. Select Filter > Blur > Gaussian Blur... Enter a blur radius of 4 pixels and click OK.

12. CTRL/CMD-click on the Chrome-1 layer in the Layers palette to select the shape. Return to the Channels palette and select Chrome-2. This will leave some blurring outside of the selection, but that is fine.

13. Choose Select > Inverse.

14. Go to Edit > Fill... In the Fill dialog select Black and choose 100% in Normal mode.

15. Go to Select > Inverse again to reselect the shape.

16. To enhance the effect we are creating, the white/black contrast needs a clearer definition, as this directly affects the steps that follow. Go to Image > Adjustments > Brightness/Contrast... Enter the following settings and click OK:

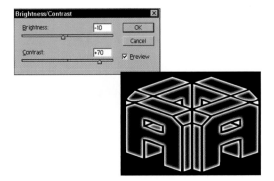

17. Hit CTRL/CMD+D to deselect.

18. Go back to the Layers palette. Select the Chrome-1 layer.

19. Choose Filter > Render > Lighting Effects... Enter the settings as shown below:

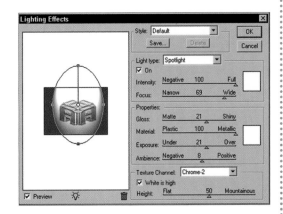

20. Next, go to Image > Adjustments > Curves... Create a curve as close to this screenshot as possible.

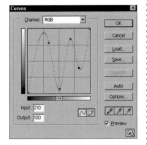

21. Go ahead and click on the eye for the Background layer to make it visible again. Note how using the blurred channel for the lighting effects has enhanced not only the reflection on the object, but imposed bevels around the edges.

22. Duplicate the shape layer (Chrome-1). Rename the duplicate layer to 'Chrome-2'.

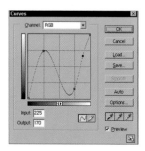

23. Choose Image > Adjustments > Curves (CTRL/CMD+M). Duplicate the curve seen below as closely as possible.

24. Take a look at the image below. The curve intensifies the metallic sheen and faux reflection.

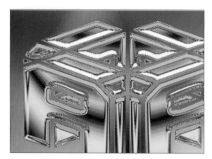

25. CTRL/CMD-click the Chrome-2 layer in the Layers palette to generate a selection of the shape.

26. Select Filter > Blur > Gaussian Blur. Enter a blur radius of 3.5 pixels. Click OK.

27. In the Layers palette, set the Blending Mode for Chrome-2 to Multiply. Decrease the opacity of the layer to 80%.

28. With Chrome-2 selected, go to Layer > Merge Down or hit CTRL/CMD+E to merge Chrome-2 into Chrome-1.

29. Hit CTRL/CMD+M to open the CURVES dialog. Enter a curve setting like the one seen here, and click OK.

The next image shows the state of the image thus far. Note that the work performed on the original shape has taken on an almost sterling silver quality that practically shines!

30. The edges of the shape have a rough appearance, but a little layer style manipulation will help take care of that. Click the 'Add a Layer Style' icon on the bottom of the Layers palette. Select Stroke from the menu, and enter a stroke with the following attributes:

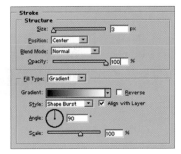

31. Select Bevel and Emboss from the left side menu in the Layer Style dialog box. Enter the following bevel settings:

This next Layer Style setting is going to help turn the silver into gold.

32. Select Inner Glow from the left-hand menu. For the color of the glow, click in the color box to open the Color Picker dialog box. Enter a color setting of R=247, G=179 and B=16. Modify the Inner Glow settings as follows:

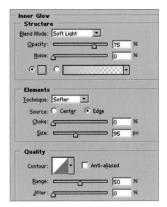

Here's the image so far. Note that the stroke applied in the last steps has effectively wiped away the jaggedness of the shape's edges.

33. Select the Background layer and click on the 'Add a Layer' icon. This creates a new layer beneath the Chrome-1 layer.

34. Select the Chrome-1 layer. Using Layer > Merge Down, merge the Chrome-1 layer with the empty layer beneath it.

35. Select Filter > Render > Lighting Effects. We want to enter the following settings in the dialog box.

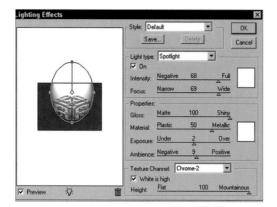

Take a look at where we're at now:

36. CTRL/CMD-click the shape layer to generate the selection again. Now select the background layer. Add a new layer in the Layers palette, and go to Edit > Fill. Use Black as the fill color; set it to 80% opacity.

37. CTRL/CMD+D to deselect. We'll now apply a blur, using Filter > Blur > Gaussian Blur. Set a blur radius of 15 pixels, and click OK.

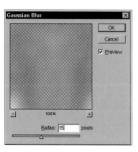

The desired effect we are trying to achieve is to create a drop shadow, but one that matches the direction of the lighting. In this instance the light is hitting the object from a 90-degree angle, but appears to be relatively close to the top surface of the object. The Layer Style drop shadow doesn't work in this instance. Even now, the shadow can be tweaked to better fit the object's shape and lighting.

38. Go to Edit > Transform > Distort. Move the Transform points in such a way that the shadow opposes the light source. This may require some careful scrutiny. When satisfied, click the Commit Transform icon in the options bar. This is found on the right side of the bar, appearing as a checkmark.

39. In the Layers palette, create a new copy of the Chrome-1 layer.

40. With the new player selected, go to Image > Adjustments > Desaturate or hit CTRL/CMD+SHIFT+U.

41. Now select Image > Adjustments > Hue/Saturation, and enter the following settings in the dialog box:

Here's our metal text, but with a gold hue:

42. CTRL/CMD-click the shape layer again to generate the selection.

43. To add to the realism, we're going to add some tarnish to the metal surface. Select the Polygonal Lasso tool. In the options bar, set the following attributes for the tool:

The tarnish will be applied to the lower portion of the shape, so the upper portion of the selection needs to be removed. For this example the shape is somewhat 3-dimensional, so the deleted selection needs to reflect that.

Here's the remaining selection:

44. In the Layers palette, create a new layer at the top of the layer stack. Hit the D key to reset the default colors (Black foreground, White background).

45. Select the Gradient tool. In the options bar, set the gradient as Foreground to Transparent, and the other attributes as follows:

46. Starting just above the centerline of the shape, draw the gradient straight down to the lowest edge of the selection.

47. Let's add some noise. Go to Filter > Noise > Add Noise, and set the amount to 70%, the Distribution to Uniform and ensure that the Monochromatic option is checked. Apply the effect by clicking OK.

48. In the Layers palette, set the Blending Mode for the gradient layer to Overlay, and the Opacity to 50%.

Here's the effect that the noise achieves:

49. We are almost there! Select Filter > Brush Strokes > Spatter, and input the following settings:

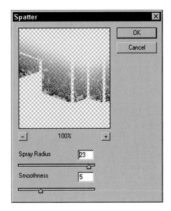

Let's add another blur. Choose Filter > Blur > Motion Blur, and assign the angle and distance values as follows:

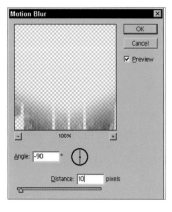

Here's our newly gilded shape, complete with reflections, shadows, and tarnish.

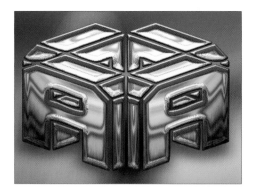

2: Springs

Photo realistic metal objects are actually fairly easy to create in Photoshop once you have a handle on creating the shape and lighting the object. As seen in the first tutorial, metal effects can be used to give depth to a flat object within a layer. What if the object you're creating rotates about a central point? This tutorial tackles this problem of rendering a 3D object in a 2D program by creating a spring.

1. To start, create a new image with the following attributes:

2. Go to Edit > Fill, and set the attributes as follows:

3. Create a new layer in the Layers palette, and then set the Foreground Color to Gray.

4. Choose the Shape tool and set the options bar attributes as follows:

5. Draw a pill button shape in the new layer.

6. CTRL/CMD-click the shape layer to generate a selection of the button. Now set the foreground color to light gray and the background to dark gray.

7. Choose the Gradient tool and set the options bar attributes as follows for a Foreground to Background gradient:

8. Starting at the center of the pill selection, draw the gradient to the bottom edge of the selection. The gradient needs to be applied totally perpendicular to the bottom edge of the selection.

9. Hit CTRL/CMD+D to deselect the shape.

10. Duplicate the shape layer.

11. Select the Move tool and use the arrow keys to move the duplicate pill button vertically. Holding the SHIFT key while moving with the arrow keys increases the amount of pixels to 5 per click. Once the button is above the other by at least half a length, CTRL/CMD-click the duplicate layer in the Layers palette to generate a selection around the button.

12. Go to Edit > Transform > Rotate, and, in the options bar, set the angle of the rotation to 15 degrees. Next, click the Accept Change icon.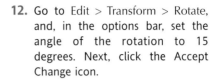

13. Use Select > Deselect to remove the button selection.

14. Now duplicate the layer you just applied the transform to and select the duplicate layer.

15. Rotate once more, this time by -30 degrees, and click the Accept Change icon.

Here's the effect this rotation will result in:

16. Once again, use the Move tool and the arrow keys to move the selected layer so that the two ends of the buttons overlap.

17. Select the layer one down from the top and choose the Burn tool. We'll use this tool to darken areas, effectively blending the pieces together to appear as though they are one continuous piece. Use a round feathered brush, and set the following attributes for the Burn tool in the options bar:

18. Increase the zoom on the image to help refine your strokes while burning, and run the Burn tool in circular strokes around the edge of the pill shape.

19. Select the top layer and then merge the two shape layers together. Create a copy of the newly merged layer. Now use the Move tool and the arrow keys to position the layer so the spring appears to have another rotation.

20. Duplicate the layer twice more, moving each layer to create a new rotation.

21. We have left Layer 2 alone for quite some time, but it's time to give it some attention again. Select Layer 2 in the Layers palette; it should be positioned just above the background layer.

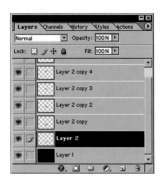

22. Go to Edit > Transform > Distort. In the Width box in the options bar, set the width to 60% and click the Accept Change icon. Using the Move tool, position the pill button so that it, too, joins with the spring on the right-hand side.

23. Select the Elliptical Marquee tool and ensure that Normal Mode is selected in the options bar. Select the tip of the button on the left side and delete it.

24. Make a smaller selection with the Marquee tool on the same tip. Ensure it does not exceed the upper and lower edges of the pill shape. Now use the Gradient tool, with Foreground to Background selected in the toolbar, to fill the selection from left to right.

25. Deselect the current selection, then duplicate Layer 2 and place it at the top of the layer stack in the Layers palette. Go to Edit > Transform > Distort and again enter a width of 60%. Click the 'Accept Change' icon to confirm the change. With the Move tool, move the shape to the top of the spring so that it joins with the end of the spring.

26. Note the contrast between the two pieces. Use the Blur tool with a small, soft brush, to blur the right edge so that it appears to blend with the other piece.

Here's where we're at:

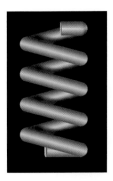

27. Starting with the top layer, repeatedly use Layer > Merge Down until all layers except the background are merged together. Name the merged layer as 'Spring-1'.

28. Go to Image > Adjustments > Curves. Enter a curve setting that resembles that of the image below as closely as possible. If your curve doesn't quite match the example (if you accidentally add too many points), ALT-click the cancel button to reset the curve without closing the dialog box and try again.

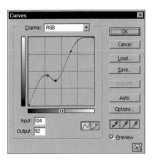

Here's the metallic sheen the curve setting applies to the spring.

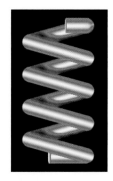

29. Time to add some tarnish to this extremely clean object. Duplicate the Spring-1 layer. Go to Filter > Brush Strokes > Spatter and enter the following settings in the Spatter dialog box:

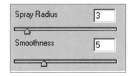

30. Set the Blending Mode for the spattered layer to Overlay and the Opacity to 50%. Now merge the spattered layer with the Spring-1 layer.

31. We'll now use the Burn tool again with a soft, circular brush. Keep the size as 13 pixels, the range as Highlights and the exposure as 50%, like we used previously. Run the Burn tool around the curved edges of the spring, as in the screenshot. Also add spots along the facing side of the spring.

32. CTRL/CMD-click the Spring-1 layer to generate a selection of the spring.

33. Create a new layer above the spring. Now click on the foreground color to open the Color Picker dialog and enter a color value of R=149, G=111, and B=70. Go to Edit > Fill, and using the foreground color set to 100% opacity, fill the selection.

34. Select Filter > Noise > Add Noise and set the attributes as follows: Uniform, 20%, Monochromatic. Click OK.

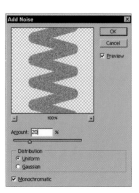

35. Once again, go to Filter > Brush Strokes > Spatter Enter the following settings in the Spatter dialog box:

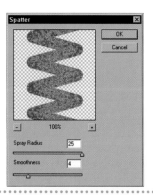

36. Set the Layer Blending Mode for the spattered layer to Overlay and the Opacity to 70%.

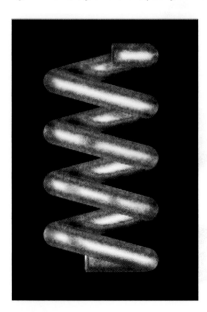

Although many metal effects seem as though they take a long time to master, actually they're some of the easiest to conquer. Why? Well, the color palette is dramatically reduced from other effects, as shades of gray are the primary ingredient. Possibly the most difficult aspects are mastering the gradients and reflections. Those can be trying, but taking a look at how light and shadow play on real-world objects can help to understand where they should be enhanced in your art.

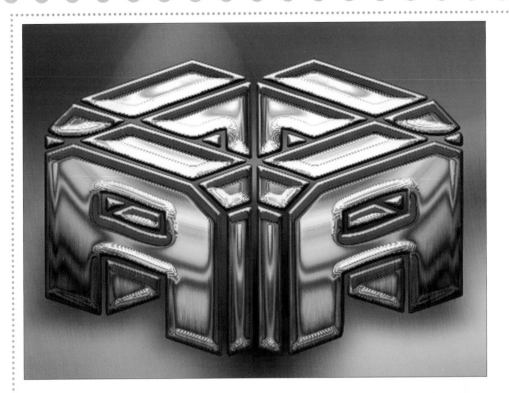

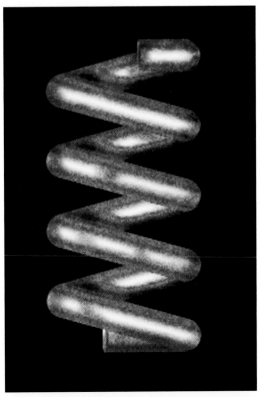

Chapter 2

Glass, Plastic, and Transparencies

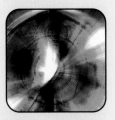

Another of the more popular requests both Colin and I receive deals with the process of creating realistic glass and plastic. Before I begin, let me say this right up front: realism in glossy, transparent objects doesn't rest in how transparent they are. The secret, if it is indeed a hidden truth, rests in the manner in which light and shadow plays on, through, and behind the object. Indeed, this can be said about metal to a degree, though metal objects lean more toward gradient structure rather than reflection and refraction.

As we go into the following tutorials, keep the above statement in mind. I'll start with a simple sphere and move on to more complex combinations of shapes, but always pay attention to the light. Light is your friend.

1: Glass sphere

> *Special thanks are due to Steven Cortez for allowing us to use of some of his incredible images! For more information on his fantastic images and how to acquire them for your own work, visit his web site at www.imagedesigning.com.*

1. To begin, open `Artwork66.jpg`, found in the `Chapter_01` folder on the CD.

2. Go to Image > Image Size. Set the dimensions for `Artwork66.jpg` to the following in the dialog box:

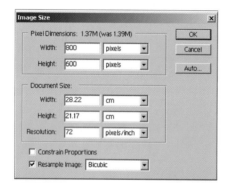

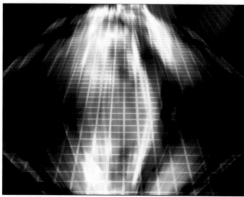

3. The base image will be used to generate the sphere. First we need a circular selection. Select the Elliptical Marquee tool and enter the following settings for the tool in the options bar:

4. Make a large circular selection in the middle of the image.

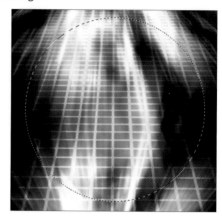

5. Go to Layer > New > Layer via Copy. This pastes another instance of the selected area into a new layer above the background. This will be the foundation of our glass sphere.

6. In the Layers palette, rename the new layer 'Base Sphere'.

7. When the circle was pasted into the new layer, the selection became inactive. CTRL/CMD-click the Base Sphere layer in the Layers palette to generate the selection once more.

8. Choose Filter > Distort > Spherize In the Spherize dialog box, ensure the settings are as follows:

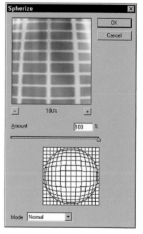

Here's the result of this filter:

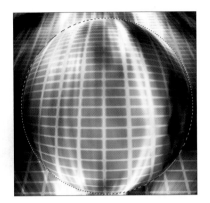

9. Duplicate the Base Sphere layer, naming the copy 'Second Sphere'. Now create an empty layer at the top called 'Large Highlight'.

10. Select the Rectangular Marquee tool. In the options bar, set the attributes as follows:

11. Select the lower two-thirds of the active selection to delete it from the current selection.

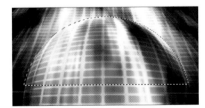

12. Hit the D key to reset the default foreground and background colors, then hit the X key to swap them, placing white in the foreground.

13. Select the Gradient tool and set a Foreground to Transparent gradient as follows:

14. Starting at the top center of the selection, draw the gradient straight down **almost** to the bottom of the selection.

15. Go to Select > Deselect to remove the selection.

16. Choose Edit > Transform > Perspective, and then drag the point on the bottom left of the transform area towards the center of the image.

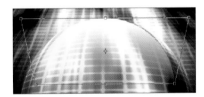

17. Click the Accept Change icon in the options bar to confirm the change.

18. In the Layers palette, create a new layer and rename it 'Side Highlight'.

19. Select the Rectangular Marquee tool again. Use the same attributes as last time, except for changing the selection type to 'New selection'.

20. Along the left-hand side of the sphere, create a rectangular selection similar to the one here:

21. In the options bar, change the selection type to 'Subtract from selection'.

22. Still using the Rectangular Marquee tool, remove portions of the selection. In this example, a narrow bar was removed vertically and two horizontally from the selection, leaving a window-style selection.

23. Go to Edit > Fill and set the options as follows:

24. Deselect the current selection and CTRL/CMD-click on the Base Sphere layer to select the sphere. Once you've done this you'll see something like this:

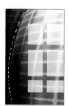

25. Now go to Filter > Distort > Spherize and enter 80% in the Amount box.

26. Deselect the sphere once again. Select the Elliptical Marquee tool in 'New selection' mode, and on the Side Highlights layer, draw a circular selection that includes the lower right portion of the side highlights as seen below. Hit the DELETE key.

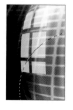 

27. Deselect the selected ellipse and then use the Move tool to position the highlights along the side of the sphere where you think they best fit the curve of the face. You may want to rotate the layer a bit to conform to the shape more realistically. To do this, go to Edit > Transform > Rotate. Grab a corner of the transform selection and move it accordingly, until the shape falls into place on the sphere's surface. When you're happy with the appearance, click the Accept Change icon on the options bar.

28. The highlights are a bit stark, but we can correct that so that they blend with the overall reflection better. With the Side Highlights layer selected in the Layers palette, CTRL/CMD-click the Side Highlights layer to generate a selection.

29. Click the 'Add layer mask' icon on the bottom of the palette, and hit D to reset the default colors, and then X to put white in the foreground. Select the Gradient tool, and in the options bar, select the Foreground to Background gradient.

30. In the Layers palette, select the mask for the Side Highlights layer. Draw the gradient across the selection, from left to right. The mask will fade the fill on the right side, helping to blend the reflection to the sphere.

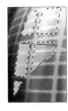

31. After deselecting the mask, select the Second Sphere layer. Change the blending mode in the Layers palette to Multiply.

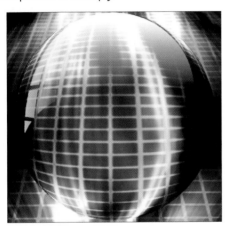

32. CTRL/CMD-click the Second Sphere layer to generate a selection of the sphere.

33. Time to add a few refractive characteristics to the glass. Select the Dodge tool and, in the options bar, set the brush to Soft Round 100 pixels, the Range to Shadows and the Exposure to 72%.

34. Select the Base Sphere layer and run the Dodge tool along the lower edge of the selection shown in the screenshot below. Do not apply too liberally just enough to lighten spot areas.

35. Select the Second Sphere layer and highlight the same areas with the Dodge tool.

36. We'll now turn to the Burn Tool. In the options bar, choose the Soft Round 65 pixels brush, with the Range set to Highlights and the Exposure to 50%. At the very bottom of the sphere, darken the area next to the selection on the Second Sphere layer.

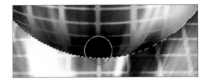

37. Deselect the sphere again. One cool way to add character to the object is to place it on a flat surface. Select the Background layer and, using the Rectangular Marquee tool, select the bottom quarter of the Background layer. (The Marquee tool should be set to 'New selection', 0 Feather value and Normal style.)

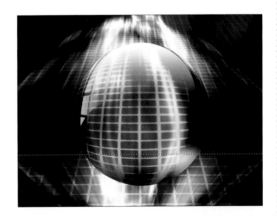

38. Go to Layer > New > Layer via Copy and name the new layer 'Floor'.

39. Now let's make it a bit more like a floor. Go to Edit > Transform > Perspective and click on the transform point on the lower right corner of the transform selection; drag it beyond the border of the image. The point on the other side will move in the opposite direction an equal distance.

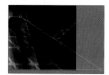

40. Click the 'Confirm transform' icon in the options bar to confirm the change.

We can enhance the glassy effect by adding a second image to the mix. The thought here is to see not only the background through the sphere, but also reflections of yet another pattern on the face of the sphere, located behind the person viewing the object.

41. Open Artwork21.jpg from the CD.

42. Go to Select > All and then Edit > Copy. Now close Artwork21.jpg and go back to the sphere image.

43. Select the Second Sphere layer. Go to Edit > Paste and the copied image will be pasted into a new layer above Second Sphere.

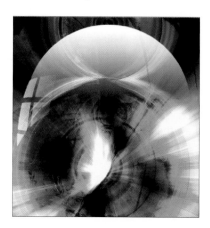

44. CTRL/CMD-click the Second Sphere layer to generate the sphere selection, and then invert the selection (Select > Inverse). Hit the DELETE key to remove the selected area.

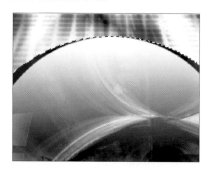

45. Invert the selection again to regain the sphere selection. Now go to Filter > Distort > Spherize and enter the Amount to 100%, with the Mode set to Normal.

46. On the Layers palette, click on the 'Add layer mask' icon.

47. Hit the D key to reset the foreground and background colors.

48. Select the Gradient tool and, in the options bar, click on the gradient window to open the Gradient Editor. Create a Black to White gradient as seen below.

49. Change the gradient style to Radial Gradient. Next, select the sphere and the layer mask and draw the Gradient from left to right through it.

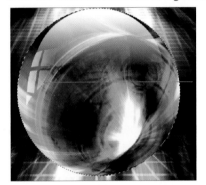

Here's the effect of the masked gradient on the sphere:

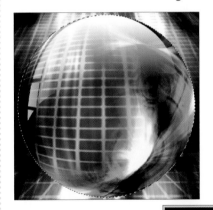

50. Set the opacity of Layer 1 to 50% in the Layers palette.

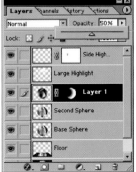

51. Now deselect the sphere once more. It's time to merge all of the sphere elements into a single layer. Select the Base Sphere layer and click the 'Create a new layer' icon. We do this because in order to collapse the layer and make the style permanent, it must be merged with an empty layer. The style is no longer editable then, but is permanently applied to the layer.

52. Select the topmost layer and use Layer > Merge Down **on each layer** until all the sphere layers reside in a single layer. When Photoshop asks you to preserve the layer mask, hit Apply.

Here's the image after the merge:

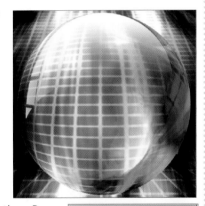

53. Duplicate the Base Sphere layer and move the copy beneath the original Base Sphere layer, just above the Floor layer. Now select the Base Sphere copy layer.

54. Go to Edit > Transform > Distort and change the Height value to 20% in the options bar. Accept this transformation. Using the Move tool, position the distorted layer so that it appears below the sphere as a shadow/reflection on the floor surface.

55. In the Layers palette, change the blending mode for the layer to Multiply.

I don't believe I've ever seen a perfect sphere: most have some distinguishing flaw or attribute to set them apart from others. Let's add a few flaws to the glass, adding not only character but enhancing the realism of the effect.

56. Duplicate the Base Sphere layer and rename the duplicate 'Bubble-1'.

57. Go to Edit > Transform > Scale. Using the transform points, shrink the layer so that it appears no larger than a marble. Click the Accept Change icon to confirm the scaling. Using the Move tool, place the small sphere somewhere on the face of its larger twin.

58. A bubble in a piece of glass is actually an open area. As a result it has its own surface, which reflects the opposite to that of the outside of the sphere. Go to Edit > Transform > Flip Vertical. Set the layer blending mode to Vivid Light, and lower the opacity of the layer to 60%.

59. Duplicate the bubble layer several times, resizing each copy and distorting the layers with the transform tools. Try changing layer opacities and blending modes of the layers to give the illusion of depth.

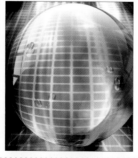

60. Select the Base Sphere layer, and set the following attribute for the Dodge tool:

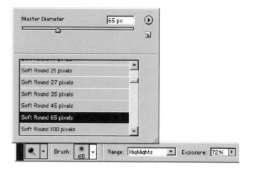

61. Using the Dodge tool, highlight the point where the sphere meets the platform.

62. Continuing with the Dodge tool, spot highlight areas where it seems the light plays best/brightest. In the example seen below, the area where the blue overlayed image seems to be centered looks as though it's a point where the light would be magnified coming through the glass and, as a result, was highlighted with the Dodge tool.

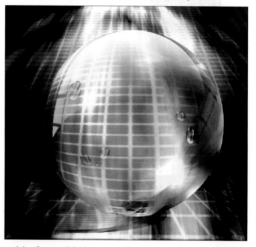

As stated before, this is more than merely a tutorial on creating cool glass. I hope you noted the process of generating the reflections and refractions, as they are key to the effect. The image used for the foundation isn't important; this sphere could have been made from a photograph of cinderblock and still looked good, thanks to a few tricks in lighting.

2: Layered plastic effects

To continue our experiment in glossy effects, let's take a look at the options available to us via **Layer Styles**. I've said it before and I'll say it again, these are the coolest tools since powdered toast! Since including custom Layer Styles for download on my website, the traffic of ActionFx.com has increased threefold, and continues to rise on a weekly basis. The bandwidth charges are killing me, but I'm told artists rarely seek wealth.

1. To begin, open `Al_Background2.jpg` from the CD.

2. Create a new layer above the Background layer, and also duplicate the Background layer.

3. With the Eyedropper tool, take a sample of the dark blue in the center of the Background copy layer. Hit the X key to swap the foreground and background colors. Again, use the Eyedropper tool to sample the light blue in the center of the Background copy layer. You should now have light blue in the foreground and dark blue in the background.

4. Click on the Gradient tool and select a Foreground to Background gradient with the following attributes:

5. With the Background copy layer active, click a point in the center of the layer and draw the gradient to either the left or right side of the image.

6. Now select a point in the center of the image and draw a gradient up or down to the edge of the image.

7. Change the foreground color to orange, and continue drawing the gradient in the Difference mode through the Background copy layer both horizontally and vertically several times, until you have something that resembles the image below. There is no way to generate this result exactly, but a few passes of the gradient should give a fairly close rendering.

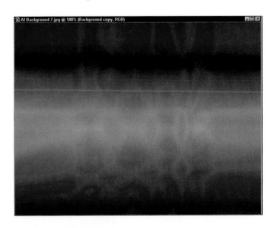

8. Click on the Horizontal Type Mask tool. In the options bar, choose your font (any will do, but large thick fonts work best). For this example I've chosen a font named Hominis, downloaded from a free font server on the Internet.

9. In the center of the Background copy layer, type your text.

10. The next step is to go to Layer > New > Layer via Copy and name the new layer 'Type Base'. It's time to apply our first Layer Style, so click on the 'Add a layer style' icon in the Layers palette.

11. From the Layer Style menu that opens, choose Bevel and Emboss. In the Bevel and Emboss dialog box, enter the following settings:

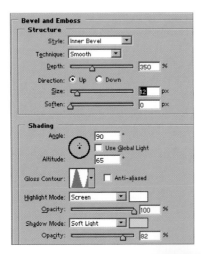

12. Without closing the Layer Styles dialog box, take a look at your text. It has already taken on glass/plastic qualities by adjusting the settings in this one dialog box.

13. Return to the Layer Styles dialog box, and in the left-hand menu select Inner Shadow. Enter the following settings:

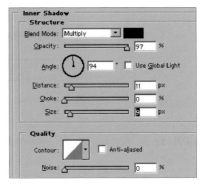

14. Now choose Drop Shadow from the left-hand menu. Enter the following settings:

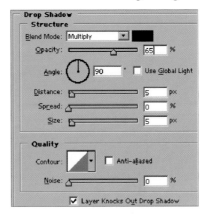

15. Next choose Inner Glow from the left-hand menu and enter the following settings:

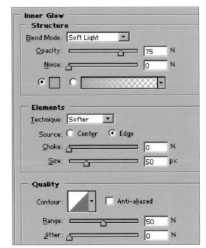

16. Now click OK to confirm all these changes. The style for this layer is now complete; go to Select > Deselect.

17. Something I've learned from Colin is that a crazy background adds to the overall effect of the design. Let's get crazy with our background by selecting the Background copy layer and, in the Layers Palette, change the blending mode to Difference.

Here's the result of this:

Don't tell Colin I said this, but I find that he's correct on more occasions then I care to admit. Go figure!

18. CTRL/CMD-click the type layer in the Layers palette to generate a selection of the text.

19. Remember that layer that we created in the beginning of this tutorial, but didn't touch? We'll get to that now. Click on Layer 1 in the Layers palette.

20. Change the foreground color to gray, and go to Edit > Stroke. In the Stroke dialog box enter the following settings:

21. Use Select > Deselect to remove the text selection. The text now has a gray outline surrounding the perimeter of the type.

22. To give the outline a character that matches its plastic text, you need only to click on and drag the Layer Style from the text layer to the outline layer.

Here's where we're at:

23. Using elements we've already generated in the previous layers, let's add one more level to our type. Click on the type layer in the Layers palette, and then CTRL/CMD-click the layer to generate the type selection.

24. Go to Select > Modify > Contract and enter a value of 12 pixels.

25. Now copy the selection to a new layer via Layer > New > Layer via Copy. A smaller version of the plastic type, complete with Layer Style, has now been placed above the type layer adding another dimension to the text. To separate the new layer from the old even further, go to Image > Adjustments > Hue/Saturation and enter the following settings:

Take a look at the image now:

Whoever said that Layer Styles couldn't be fun and effective in designing special effects? Don't be one of the naysayers and pass them off too quickly. Just because they're easy to make and quick to apply doesn't make them less effective in stylish design. Try them on buttons, interfaces and logos. Enjoy!

3: Chromed glass

The final tutorial in this chapter on things reflective gives a new twist to the process of creating chrome effects. With a few subtle variations, the process of creating chrome can also be used for generating glass and reflections that will stun your friends and cohorts. I'm stunned just thinking about it!

1. To begin, create a new image named Chromed Glass. Set the attributes for the new image as follows:

2. Start by going to Edit > Fill and select Black, 100% Opacity as the fill color.

3. Now create a new layer, and then select the Custom Shape tool. Set the following attributes for the Paw shape, which can be found in the Animals shape set in the Photoshop Shapes Directory:

4. Click the mouse in the upper left portion of the image and drop a large paw in the center by dragging the mouse to the lower right portion of the image. The shape will fill with your foreground color, but as we will delete it, this foreground color doesn't matter.

5. CTRL/CMD-click the paw layer to generate a selection around the paw, and then hit the DELETE key.

6. Now open the Fill dialog again (Edit > Fill...), entering the following settings:

7. Now go to the Channels palette and create a new channel. This will be called 'Alpha 1'.

8. Once again, go to Edit > Fill. This time we'll use White as the fill color, with the opacity set to 50%. This will give the appearance of a gray fill, though it will actually be semi-transparent.

9. Return to the Layers palette and create a new layer. Reopen the Fill dialog box and set the fill color to gray, with the opacity as 100%.

10. Switch back to the Channels palette again and select Alpha-1. Use Select > Deselect to remove the current selection. Let's apply a blur at this point. Go to Filter > Blur > Gaussian Blur and enter a blur radius of 2 pixels.

11. Go to Select > Reselect to regenerate our last selection.

12. Back in the Layers palette, select Layer 3.

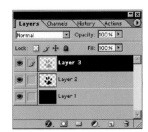

13. Let's apply some lighting effects, by means of Filter > Render > Lighting Effects. We'll use the following settings:

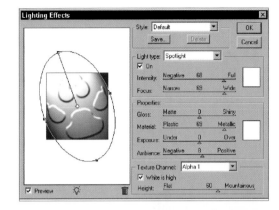

When you click OK, here's the effect you'll see:

14. Returning to the Channels palette, select the RGB Channel.

15. We'll now apply a Curves adjustment to the RGB channel. Go to Image > Adjustments > Curves. In the Curves dialog box, enter a curve similar to the one represented here:

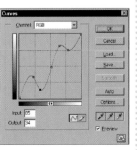

16. After clicking OK to confirm the curve, return to the Layers palette and select Layer 3.

17. Again, go to Image > Adjustments > Curves and enter a curve similar to the one here.

18. Click OK and you should see something like this:

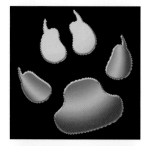

19. Duplicate Layer 3, and then apply the Chrome filter (Filter > Sketch > Chrome), with the Detail set to 6 and the Smoothness to 4.

20. Set the layer blending mode for Layer 3 copy to Overlay.

Take a look at the effect of this blending mode:

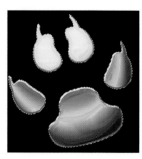

21. Create a new copy of Layer 3 and place it below Layer 3 copy. Again, go to Filter > Sketch > Chrome. This time set the Detail to 6 and the Smoothness to 10. Set the layer blending mode for this layer to Overlay as well.

22. It's now time to add some chrome color to the paw. Click on the foreground color, and in the Color Picker dialog box, enter a color value of #B8F2EE. Enter a color value of #B99D68 for the background color.

23. Create a new layer and place this new layer at the top of the layer stack in the Layers palette.

24. Let's turn now to the Gradient tool. In the options bar click on the gradient window – the Gradient Editor will appear. Choose the Foreground to Background gradient and drag the color sliders towards the center as illustrated below:

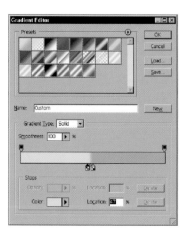

25. Back on the options bar, select the following options for the tool:

26. Starting from the top of the paw down to the bottom of the selection, fill the layer with the gradient.

27. Go to Filter > Distort > Wave and enter the following setting in the resulting dialog box:

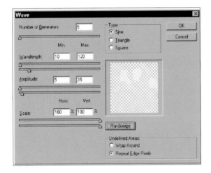

28. Once you've applied these wave settings, return to the Layer palette and set the blending mode for the selected layer to Overlay.

29. We've added a wave effect; now let's add a ripple. Go to Filter > Distort > Ripple and set the Ripple Amount to 330, and the Size to Medium. Follow the ripple up with a Gaussian Blur with a blur radius of 6 pixels (Filter > Blur > Gaussian Blur). Now deselect the current selection with Select > Deselect.

Up to this point the paw looks pretty metallic. But wait, this is a chapter on glass! Not to worry my friends. If it's glass you want, then glass you shall have.

30. In the Layers palette select Layer 3, and then go to Image > Adjustments > Curves. Create a curve similar to the one here:

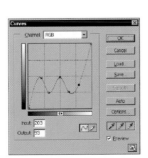

31. Select Layer 3 copy 2, and apply a curve to this as well. Make this curve as close as you can get to the one shown here:

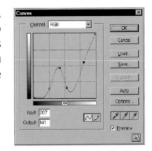

Do you see it? The glass effect is now becoming apparent.

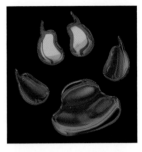

32. Now select Layer 3 copy, and once again apply a curve.

33. We'll now make a duplicate of Layer 4 and place it at the top of the layer stack. This enhances the color applied to the glass.

Here's the result of our curves:

34. The paw is starting to look pretty glassy, but we can do better than that. On the CD, find and open the image `Artwork44.jpg`. Rotate the image 90 degrees clockwise (Image > Rotate Canvas > 90° CW).

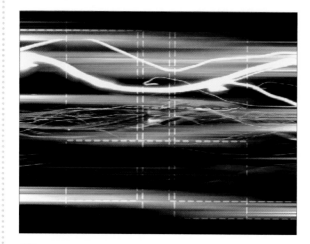

35. Now select the image (Select > All) and copy it (Edit > Copy). Close `Artwork44.jpg` at this point and return to your glass effect.

36. Select Layer 1 and Edit > Paste here to insert the Artwork image. Set the layer opacity for the pasted layer to 5%.

Your glass paw should be developing nicely.

37. Now select the topmost layer in the palette, Layer 4 copy. Paste another copy of the Artwork image here, and set the layer blending mode of the new layer to Overlay, with opacity of 75%.

38. Time to brighten this up a bit before we close out this tutorial. Select Layer 2, which holds the original paw shape. Click on the 'Add a layer style' icon, and select Outer Glow from the menu. Enter a glow setting as follows:

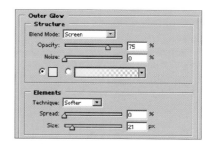

The image below shows the resulting glass, created using metal techniques.

Chapter 3

Eco-friendly Effects

Nature has always been a major contributor to art. Inspiration is derived from the patterns, textures, and lighting we see around us. Some artists use material found in nature as a basis for their work. A huge tree was snapped off close to the base in my neighborhood – a local sculptor used a chainsaw to turn the stump into a grizzly bear.

This chapter takes two approaches to applying nature to art. We'll use natural textures and photographs for implementation in our images, as well as incorporating natural elements in images from scratch, using only the tools given to us by Adobe Photoshop.

Aged wood etching

1. To begin, rather than generate wood from scratch, we'll be using an existing photo and apply a realistic etch effect to it. Open `A1-Wood1.jpg` found on the CD. (If you are interested in learning how to create wood grain textures from scratch, Photoshop Most Wanted volume 1 tells you how to go about it.)

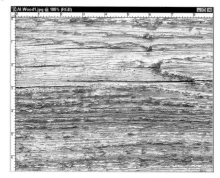

2. Click the 'Create a new layer' icon at the bottom of the Layers palette. Name the new layer 'Base Shape'.

3. Hit the D key to reset the default colors in the foreground and background. Go to the toolbox and click on the Custom Shape tool. In the options bar, click on the 'Fill pixels' icon. Ensure that Mode is set to Normal and Opacity to 100%.

4. The Custom Shape options bar has a window called Shape. Click the small arrow to the right of the Shape window to open and view the shapes available. The shape used in this tutorial is called World, and found in the Symbols shape set. This set may not be loaded yet, so click the small arrow in the upper right corner of the Shapes palette. This opens the Shapes menu where you can select and load the Symbols shape set.

5. When loaded, choose the shape named World.

6. Draw your shape so that it is centered in the middle of the image.

7. CTRL/CMD-click the 'Base Shape' layer to generate a selection of your shape.

8. Open the Channels palette. On the bottom of the palette, click the 'Create a new channel' icon.

9. Go to Edit > Fill. In the Field dialog box, use white as the fill color. Set the opacity of the fill to 100%. Click OK.

10. Go to Select > Deselect (CTRL/CMD+D).

11. Go to Filter > Blur > Gaussian Blur. Enter a blur radius of 10 pixels. Click OK.

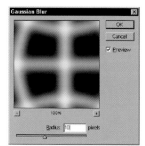

12. Go to Select > Reselect. (CTRL/CMD+SHIFT+D), and then Select > Inverse (CTRL/CMD+SHIFT+I).

13. Go to Edit > Fill. Enter black as the fill color and an opacity of 100%. Click OK. We do this to take away most of the blurred area, leaving only the shape with blurred edges. This will work to our benefit shortly.

14. Go to Select > Inverse (CTRL/CMD+SHIFT+I).

15. Select Image > Adjustments > Curves. Duplicate the curve seen in the screenshot here as closely as possible. Once done, click OK.

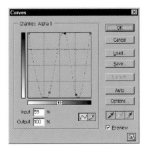

16. Select Image > Adjustments > Brightness/Contrast. Set the brightness level to –60, and the contrast to 90. Click OK.

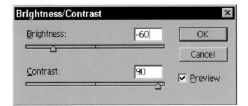

17. Go to Select > Deselect (CTRL/CMD+D).

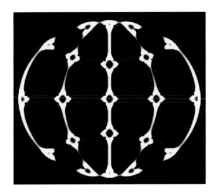

18. Return to the Layers palette. Click the eye to the left on the 'Base Shape' layer, rendering it invisible. Select the Background layer.

19. Go to Select > All (CTRL/CMD+A).

20. Hit CTRL/CMD+C to copy the selected background.

21. Hit CTRL/CMD+N to create a new image. The new image will have the same dimensions as the background copied to the clipboard. Name the new image 'displace'. Click OK. The new image will be used to create a displacement map that will force the shape into the grain of the wood. Check it out...this is very cool!

22. Hit CTRL/CMD+V to paste the copied selection into the new image.

23. Go to Image > Adjustments > Desaturate.

24. Now go to Image > Adjustments > Brightness/Contrast. Set the brightness to –20, and the contrast to +30. Click OK.

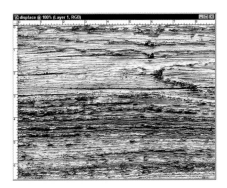

25. Select File > Save. Find a spot on your computer to save the 'displace' image as a PSD file. Remember where you put it, as we will need it shortly. Close displace.psd.

26. Return to the wood logo image. CTRL/CMD-click the 'Base Shape' layer to generate a selection in the form of the shape.

27. Select the Background layer in the Layers palette, and go to Layer > New > Layer via Copy (CTRL/CMD+J).

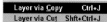

28. Right-click the new layer in the palette, or double-click the layer name to change the Layer Properties. Rename the layer 'Embedded Logo'. If you right-clicked, just click OK in the Layer Properties dialog box to accept the change; if you double-clicked the layer name, simply click on the layer once to accept the change.

29. On the Layers palette, click the 'Add a layer style' icon, and select Bevel and Emboss... from the menu.

30. In the Layer Styles dialog box, enter the following bevel settings and click OK:

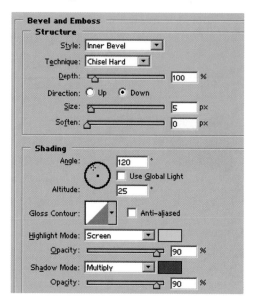

31. CTRL/CMD-click the Base Shape layer.

32. Go to Filter > Render > Lighting Effects. In the Lighting Effects dialog box, enter the following settings and click OK:

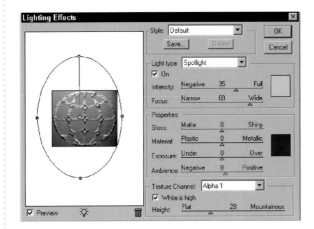

33. Hit CTRL/CMD+D to deselect. Look at the screenshot below to see the effect so far. See how easy this is? Well, maybe not easy just yet, but once you wrap your mind around the process of embedding, a whole new realm of design opens to you. Not just quick designs applied with Layer Styles, but photo-realistic engraving any whittler would be proud of.

34. Hit CTRL/CMD+SHIFT+D to reselect.

35. With the Embedded Logo layer still selected, click the 'Add layer mask' icon at the bottom of the Layers palette.

36. Go to Filter > Distort > Displace. Enter 5% as the horizontal scale. Also, enter 5% as the vertical scale. The Displacement Map and Undefined Areas settings are unimportant at this time. Click OK.

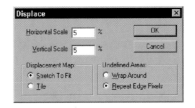

37. Photoshop will now ask you to choose a displacement map. In the 'Choose a displacement map' dialog box, find and open the displace.psd image created earlier.

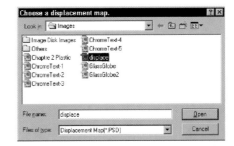

The image below shows the effect the displacement map has on the masking layer:

38. CTRL/CMD-click the masking layer. A selection is generated around the distorted mask.

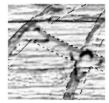

39. Go to Select > Modify > Expand. In the Expanded Selection dialog box, expand by 2 pixels and click OK.

40. Go to Filter > Distort > Displace. In the 'Displace' dialog box, enter a horizontal scale of 3%. Enter a vertical scale of 3% also. Click OK.

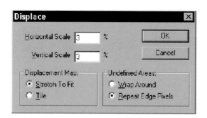

41. Again, choose the display.psd image for your displacement map. Click Open to apply the distortion to the selection on the masking layer. Hit CTRL/CMD+D to deselect.

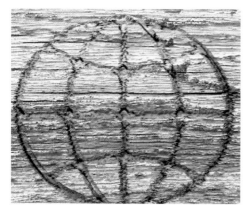

42. At the bottom of the Layers palette, click on the 'Add a layer style' icon. Choose Bevel and Emboss from the menu.

43. In the Bevel and Emboss dialog box, enter the following Bevel settings and click OK:

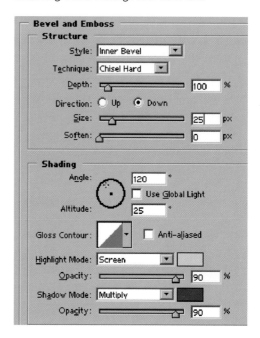

Here you see the image with the second Bevel applied:

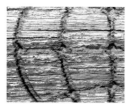

If you've made it to this point, your image should appear as though an emblem has been etched into the face of the wood at some time in the distant past. The effect can be enhanced by also applying text to the face overlapping the emblem.

44. Create a new layer above the Embedded Logo layer. Rename the new layer Faded Paint.

45. Select the Horizontal Type Mask tool from the toolbox. In the options bar, select a font to place over the logo. In this instance, I've selected a free font I found online called Ancient Geek, from Matthew Welch's site www.squaregear.net/fonts/geek.shtml. (Thanks Matthew!)

46. Set the attributes for your font in the options bar. For this example I've set the font size to 180 pts, with the anti-aliasing method set to Strong, center justified.

47. Type your wording in the new layer.

48. Click on the foreground color. Set the color to R:255, G:2, B:2,. Click OK.

49. Go to Edit > Fill. In the Fill dialog box, set the fill color to foreground, 100% opacity.

50. Go to Select > Deselect (CTRL/CMD+D).

51. Go to Edit > Transform > Rotate.

52. In the options bar, change the angle to -20 degrees.

53. Hit the 'Commit transform' icon in the options bar, or just hit ENTER to accept the transformation.

54. CTRL/CMD-click the Faded Paint layer in the Layers palette to generate a selection of the type.

55. With the selection now active, click the 'Add layer mask' icon at the bottom of the Layers palette.

56. Go to Filter > Distort > Displace. Set the horizontal scale to 4%. Set the vertical scale to 4% also. Click OK.

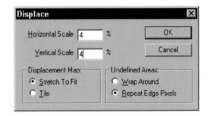

57. Again, find the displace.psd image and click Open to apply it to the mask. The paint is starting to take on a distorted, chipped quality as seen here:

58. In the Layers palette, set the blending mode for the Faded Paint layer to Darken.

59. On the bottom of the Layers palette, click the 'Add a layer style' icon. Select Blending Options... from the top of the menu.

60. At the bottom of the Blending Options dialog box, you'll see Blend If: Gray. Open the drop-down menu and change the Blend If: setting to Red. Move the Underlying Layer left-hand slider to 98. Click OK.

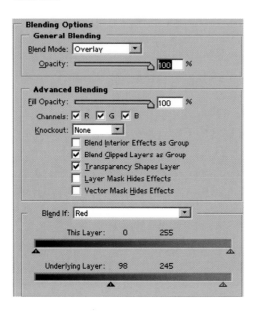

61. Change the opacity of the Faded Paint layer to 90%.

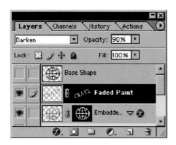

62. Click the 'Add a layer style' icon again, this time choosing Bevel and Emboss... from the menu. Enter the following settings in the Bevel and Emboss dialog box and click OK:

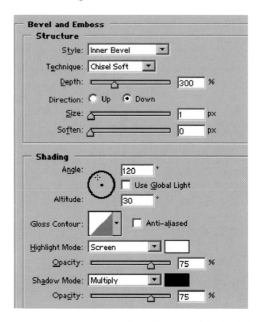

Below you can see our completed image with the faded paint that fits into the grooves of the wood:

Mixing oil and water

Of all the tutorials that I've done so far, this is perhaps one of my favorites. I must admit that this came about quite by accident. As a designer I'm always trying to find new ways to revamp effects I've already mastered, but one day I had forgotten exactly how I did the water previously. In a bind, I started messing with a few commands I hadn't used in the process before... and Oil and Water was born. One of the great things about Photoshop is that after you understand the tools and how different elements of the program work together, sometimes even your mistakes look good!

1. To begin, open `Al-Metal1.jpg` found on the CD.

2. In the Layers palette, click the 'Create a new layer' icon. Name the new layer Shape Layer 1.

3. Hit the D key to reset the foreground and background colors, placing black in the foreground.

4. Click on the Custom Shape tool. In the options bar, click the small arrow next to the Custom Shape example window. A window will open showing the shapes currently loaded into Photoshop. In the upper right corner of the

shapes window that opens is another small arrow button. Click this button and select Replace Shapes from the menu.

5. On the CD, find the custom shape set named PMW-Eyes.csh and load it into the Custom Shapes palette. Select the shape that looks like an eye with a tear running from the left corner.

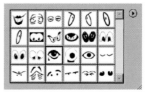

6. For the rest of the Custom Shape options, click the 'Fill pixels' icon. Set the Mode to Normal, Opacity to 100% and Anti-aliased checked.

7. Draw the shape in the new layer. To keep the shape to scale while drawing, hold the SHIFT key down. It will be filled with black automatically, as shown below.

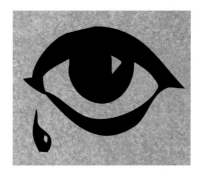

As you can see, this shape has a lot of sharp or hard edges. In order to turn this into water, we will have to do some softening and distorting.

8. In the Toolbox bar, click on the Rectangular Marquee tool. Enter the following attributes for the Rectangular Marquee tool in the options bar:

9. Click and drag the Rectangular Marquee tool around the lower half of the eye shape.

10. Go to Filter > Liquify. When the Liquify dialog box appears, you'll see that the area enclosed by the marquee is centered in the liquify field. The feather of the selection has created a soft edge where the selection meets the mask. This indicates that only the area not covered with a red hue will be subject to our edit. However, as the selection was feathered, some distortion in the blended overlap will occur if you so choose.

11. On the left of the Liquify dialog box is a vertical menu of tools specific to the Liquify filter. Click on the topmost tool, called the Warp tool.

12. On the right side of the Liquify dialog box, settings for the selected tool may be adjusted. Enter the settings shown in this screenshot:

13. The Liquify tool acts in a similar manner to the Smudge tool. By clicking and dragging portions of the shape, the Liquify tool drags the pixels with it. In this manner, distort selected areas of the shape by dragging them down, or by using the Bloat tool to spread specific areas.

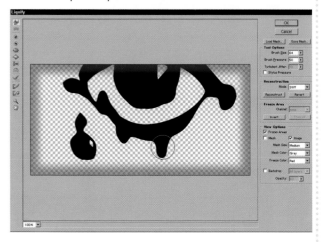

14. When you are satisfied with your distortions, click OK, and go to Select > Deselect (CTRL/CMD+D).

15. In the Toolbox, click on the Brush tool. In the options bar, set the following attributes for a hard, round brush:

16. Spray large spots of black paint onto the Shape Layer 1 layer. Just a few spots will do.

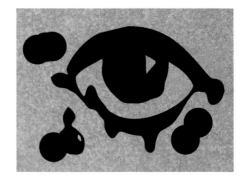

17. Once the shape and spots are in place, we can begin to transform the layer contents into liquid. At the bottom of the Layers palette, click the 'Add a layer style' icon. Select Drop Shadow from the menu that appears.

18. In the Layer Style dialog box, enter the following Drop Shadow settings:

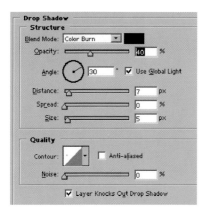

19. In the left-hand menu of the Layer Styles dialog box, select Inner Shadow. Enter the following settings:

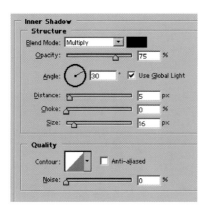

20. In the left-hand menu of the Layer Styles dialog box, select Inner Glow. Use a dark gray color, (R:103, G:103, B:101) and enter the following settings:

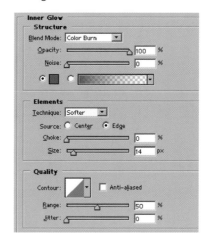

21. In the left-hand menu of the Layer Styles dialog box, select Bevel and Emboss. Use light orange (R:238, G:187, B:152) for the shadow color, and enter the following settings:

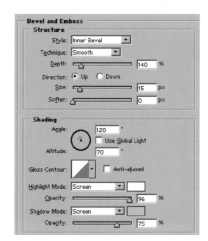

22. In the left-hand menu of the Layer Styles dialog box, select Color Overlay. Use a Blend color of gray, (R:193, G:191, B:191), and enter the following settings:

43

23. In the left-hand menu of the Layer Styles dialog box, select Gradient Overlay. Open the Gradient picker, click the little arrow to reveal the drop-down menu, and choose Load gradients... to load in PMW2-Metal1.grd, which you can find on the CD. Then enter the following settings:

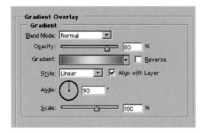

24. Before closing the Layer Style dialog box, save the style for use later in this tutorial by clicking the New Style button on the right side of the Layer Style dialog box. The style is now saved to the layer style set loaded into the Layer Styles palette. Click OK.

The shape is now taking on an almost wax-like quality.

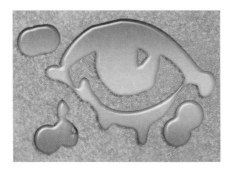

25. In the Layers palette, make a copy of the Shape Layer 1 layer. Set the opacity to 80%, and the fill amount to 80%.

26. CTRL/CMD-click the new layer in the layers palette to generate a selection.

27. Select the Shape Layer 1 layer. Click the 'Create a new layer' icon on the bottom of the Layers palette.

28. Select the Shape Layer 1 copy layer. Go to Layer > Merge Down (CTRL/CMD+E).

29. The selection should still be active. Go to Select > Modify > Contract. Enter a Contract By: setting of 16 pixels, and click OK.

30. Let's soften that selection a bit. Go to Select > Feather. Enter a Feather Radius of 6, and click OK.

31. Go to Filter > Sketch > Chrome. Enter the following settings in the 'Chrome' dialog box and click OK:

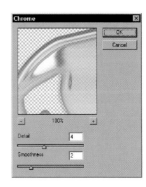

32. Go to Filter > Blur > Gaussian Blur. Enter a Radius of 4.5. Click OK.

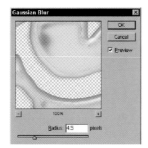

33. Go to Select > Deselect (CTRL/CMD+D). The screenshot below shows the image with the first round of chrome applied.

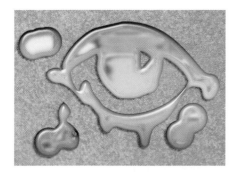

34. In the Layers palette, change the opacity and fill settings to 80%.

35. Select the Background layer and click the 'Create a new layer' icon.

36. Select the Shape Layer 1 layer in the Layers Palette. Merge Shape Layer 1 with the new layer by hitting CTRL/CMD+E.

37. Open the Layer Styles palette (Window > Styles). Click on the style saved earlier to apply it to the newly merged layer (Layer 2). You'll see the saved style as the last icon in the loaded set.

38. Select Layer 1, so named when Shape Layer 2 was merged with the empty layer. Set the blending mode to Color Burn, with an opacity of 80% and fill of 80%.

39. Go to Filter > Sketch > Chrome. In the Chrome dialog box, enter the following settings and click OK:

The image is now taking on the oil and water quality we want.

40. So how can we enhance the reflections? One way is to use the Apply Image command, which I'll demonstrate now. Open Al-Clouds2.jpg, found on the CD.

> *In order for the* Apply Image *command to work correctly, both images (source and destination) must be the same dimensions.*

41. Before we apply the image to our shape, let's rename the layers in the palette so we do not lose track of them. Change the name of Layer 2 to 'Shape Layer 1', and the name of Layer 1 to 'Shape Layer 2'. This maintains the original structure set up at the beginning of this tutorial. Once both are renamed, select Shape Layer 2.

42. CTRL/CMD-click Shape Layer 2 to generate a selection of the layer's contents.

43. Go to Image > Apply Image. Set the following attributes in the Apply Image dialog box and click OK:

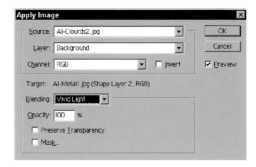

The screenshot below shows the resulting slick generated on the layer, taking on the sheen of oil on a puddle in a parking lot.

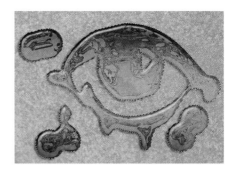

44. Can we enhance the effect? You bet. In the Layers palette, duplicate the 'Shape Layer 2' layer.

45. On the bottom of the Layers palette click the 'Add a layer style' icon. Select Bevel and Emboss from the menu. Enter the following Bevel and Emboss settings (the Gloss Contour I've used is Ring and the Shadow color is orange):

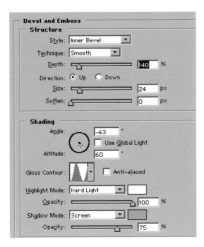

46. Click OK.

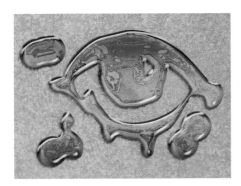

47. CTRL/CMD-click Shape Layer 2 to create a selection. Go to Filter > Distort > Displace. Enter the following settings in the Displace dialog box and click OK:

48. Once you click OK, you will be asked to find a Displacement Map. Open Ch3-RippleMap.psd, found on the CD.

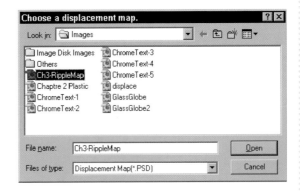

49. Click Open to apply the Displace filter to the selected layer.

50. In the Layers palette, select Shape Layer 2. Hit CTRL/CMD+F to re-run the Displace filter on Shape Layer 2.

> CMD/CTRL+F *replays the last filter used.*

51. In the Layers palette, select Shape Layer 1. Hit CTRL/CMD+F to re-run the Displace filter on Shape Layer 1.

52. Select the Background layer and click the 'Create a new layer' icon. Rename the new layer 'Stroke'.

53. In the toolbox, click on the foreground color. In the Color Picker dialog box, enter a color value of (R:131, G:130, B:130) or a number value of #838282. Click OK.

54. Go to Edit > Stroke. Enter the following settings in the Stroke dialog box and click OK:

55. Go to Select > Deselect (CTRL/CMD+D).

56. Go to Filter > Blur > Gaussian Blur. Enter a Radius of 16 pixels, and click OK.

57. Set the blending mode of the Stroke layer to Color Burn.

58. Select the Background layer. Go to Image > Adjustments > Levels. Move the sliders as shown in the screenshot below to darken the background and enhance the overall tone.

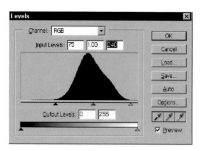

59. Click OK. And now we see the final image.

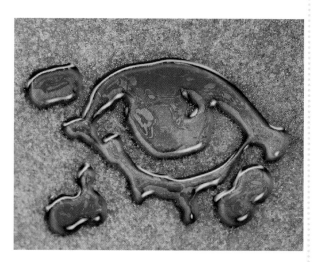

Water and oil together...they may not mix well in the real world, but they meld together in Photoshop just fine. Naturals really aren't too difficult to master, and once you have a few of the techniques down you'll be looking at your surroundings and wondering 'Hey, how do I create that type of bark? Let's see...first I would make a wood grain...'. What's more, nature can be a great inspiration for more abstract, fantasy art.

Chapter 4

Electronic Effects

Every designer making electronic effects seems to start by creating basic wiring. These tutorials are all over the Internet: stroke a path or a line, apply a colored bevel to it and distort to give it a curved or bent aspect. Hide the ends behind another layer leaving only the beveled mid section visible and you have wiring. I'm not saying this to denigrate the effect, indeed I still use it myself, but once you've learnt it, it's time to move on. This chapter is all about using these basics as a springboard to bigger and better projects.

1: Stereo cable

1. To begin, open an image to use as your background, or create a new image. You can use any background you want, but if you'd like to use the one shown here, then you'll find it on the CD, called "Wood Panels".

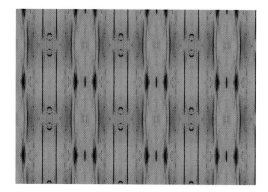

2. Click CTRL/CMD+SHIFT+N and name the layer 'Wire Coat'.

3. Select the Rectangular Marquee tool. We only want a very simple rectangle, so in the options bar choose the following options: press the 'New selection' button (on the left-hand side), don't add any feathering, and set the Style to Normal.

4. On this new layer, start from the left-hand border of the image and draw a long rectangular selection to the middle of the image.

5. Now select the Gradient tool. In the options bar, click the small arrow next to the gradient window to open the Gradient picker. For this tutorial, you'll need a specific gradient set created for this purpose. To load the gradient set in question, click the small arrow in the upper right corner of the Gradient palette. This will open the menu, at which point you should select Load Gradients.

6. Navigate to the CD and find the folder named `Gradients`. Select `PMW2-WireGrads.grd` and click Load. The new gradients will now load into the Gradient picker. Select the gradient named 'Wire Sleeve Coat'.

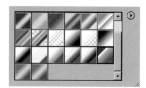

7. Select the 'Linear Gradient' setting in the options bar. Click the mouse at the top of the selection and drag it straight down to the bottom edge of the selection to fill with the gradient (holding down the SHIFT key as you do so to ensure a straight line).

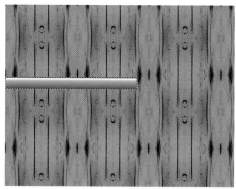

8. We're building a typical black cable, so the gradient is a bit light for our purposes. A quick Curves adjustment will correct that. Go to Image > Adjustments > Curves, (CTRL/CMD+M). Set the Input level to roughly 175%, and the Output to

around 98%. Your curve should look similar to the one below:

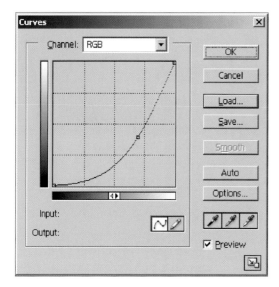

You will find my original `Cable Sections.acv` file on the CD. If you would like to use this, click the Load button in the Curves dialog and navigate to the file, then click Load again and finally hit OK to accept the adjustment.

9. When you are happy with your Curves setting, save it for future use by hitting the Save button. You will be asked to choose a folder for your curve file (extension ACV). Name the curve setting (for this example I've named it 'Cable Sections') and click OK.

Always save your settings, whatever you've created, from a simple bevel Layer Style to a Curves adjustment. You may need them later, and they are always handy to have around for other projects.

10. After clicking OK to accept the curve, deselect the shape (Select > Deselect or CTRL/CMD+D). The darker gradient fits the bill for the black cable better, and the curve not only darkens the cable, but also lightens the highlights.

11. Click CTRL/CMD+SHIFT+N to create a new layer and name it as 'Section 1'. On this layer, make a box-like selection at the right end of the cable. Fill the selection with the same gradient as before, from the top edge of the selection to the bottom.

Hold the SPACEBAR down as you are dragging out your marquee in order to move it to the desired position.

12. Go to Edit > Transform > Perspective. Select the point on the top left of the Transform bounding box and move it down to meet the corner of the cable. When in Perspective Transform mode, the bottom corner on the same side will move up to meet the bottom edge of the cable. Hit ENTER to accept the Transform settings.

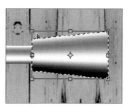

13. Let's use that curve we saved earlier. Go to Image > Adjustments > Curves. Click the Load button on the right-hand side of the Curves dialog box. Load the Cable Sections curve we created before and click OK.

14. Hit CTRL/CMD+D to deselect the current selection, and then on the same layer, use the Rectangular Marquee tool to select a narrow portion on the left side of Section 1.

15. Go to Edit > Fill to fill the area with black at 80% opacity. Click OK to confirm the fill.

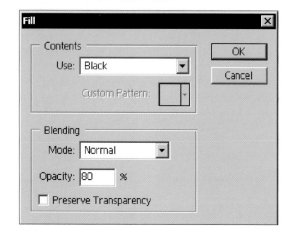

16. Deselect the current selection (CTRL/CMD +D). Now create a new layer and name it as 'Section 2'. With the Rectangular Marquee tool, make another narrow vertical selection, slightly taller than Section 1.

17. Go to Edit > Fill again, and use the same settings as last time, except for the opacity. Set this to 100%.

> *You can fill a selection with the current foreground color by clicking ALT+DELETE/BACKSPACE. To use this shortcut now, first ensure that your foreground color is set to black.*

18. Now zoom into your selection and go to Edit > Transform > Perspective. Select the point on the upper right corner of the transform selection and move the point down so that it meets the corner of Section 1. The bottom right corner will move up to meet the corresponding bottom edge of Section 1 automatically.

19. Add a further layer to the Layers palette, keeping our sequential naming by calling it 'Section 3'.

20. Make a box-like selection at the right end of Section 2. Fill the selection with the same gradient as before, from the top edge of the selection to the bottom.

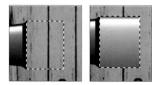

21. Once again, the gradient needs to be darker, so click CTRL/CMD+M to open the Curves dialog and then load in the curve that you saved before.

22. Click CTRL/CMD+D to remove the selection. We're now going to add some grooves to the cable. Create a new layer above Section 3 and name it 'Section 3 features'.

23. Ensure that the Rectangular Marquee tool is still selected, and set it to 'Add to selection' in the options bar. Create several small square selections as seen here:

> *Hold down the SPACEBAR while making marquee selections to reposition on the fly.*

24. Ensure that your foreground color is set to black and then click ALT+DELETE to fill the selections with 100% black.

25. We'll now want to make these grooves appear to be wrapped around the cable. To do this we'll use the Spherize filter. First CTRL/CMD-click the Section

3 layer in the Layers palette to make a selection shaped like Section 3. Then select the Section 3 features layer.

26. Go to Filter > Distort > Spherize. Change the Mode for the filter to Vertical only and move the Amount slider to 100%. Click OK to confirm the changes.

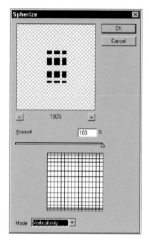

27. Now we need to create a recessed appearance for the boxes, and this can be done with a simple bevel. On the bottom of the Layers palette, click the 'Add a layer style' icon. Select Bevel and Emboss from the menu, set the direction to 'Down' and the size to roughly 5 pixels, as we only want to add a slight bevel.

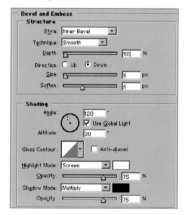

28. Click OK to confirm the bevel and then deselect the boxes. Here's the result of the bevel on the small squares pattern. The recessed appearance is now in place.

29. When building objects with several similar elements joined together, you may often utilize layers you have already made for other pieces of the object. In the Layers palette, click on Section 2. Drag the layer to the Create a new layer icon to duplicate it. Rename the duplicate as 'Section 4'.

30. Go to Edit > Transform > Flip Horizontal and then hit ENTER to accept the change. Select the Move tool and use SHIFT and the right arrow key to move Section 4 to the right side of Section 3. This will maintain the vertical alignment, while moving the section 10 pixels at a time.

31. Create a new layer at the top of the Layers palette and call it 'Section 5'. On this layer we'll make another rectangular selection as we did with Sections 3 and 2. Starting at the upper right corner of Section 4, match the left-hand side up to the right-hand side of Section 4, with the same height.

32. Repeat the process for applying the gradient and curve as done to Section 2 and Section 3.

33. Duplicate Section 4 in the Layers palette. Now use the Move tool to move the duplicate layer to the right side of Section 5.

34. We now need to resize the duplicate layer so that the left side edges match the right side edges of Section 5. Click CTRL/CMD+T, hold down the SHIFT key as you drag to retain the original proportions, and keep the ALT key held down to scale from the center of the object.

35. We're about ready to put the cable on a single layer. First, any layer with a style attached must be merged into an empty layer to collapse the style settings and commit them to the layer permanently. For this tutorial, Section 3 features has a layer style applied. Select the Section 3 layer and click on the 'Create a new layer' icon, so that a new layer appears just beneath Section 3 features.

36. Select the Section 3 features layer and go to Layer > Merge Down (CTRL/CMD+E) to merge the selected layer with the empty one below.

37. Temporarily turn off the visibility of the background layer, and then use the 'Merge Visible' command by clicking CTRL/CMD+SHIFT+E. Rename the newly merged layer as 'Cable'.

38. Create a new layer between the Cable and Background layers, naming it as 'Jack Section 1'.

39. Use the Rounded Rectangle tool with the Radius set to 5 pixels, which refers to the size of the corner radius. Make sure that you have chosen the 'Fill pixels' setting on the left-hand side of the options bar.

40. Draw a small rounded rectangle in the Jack Section 1 layer, so that the right side protrudes from behind the cable. Then CTRL/CMD-click the Jack Section 1 layer in the Layers palette to select the shape.

41. Select the Gradient tool. If the Default gradient set is not loaded, open the Gradient menu again and scroll down to Reset Gradients. In the Gradient picker, click on the Copper gradient. Fill the selection from top to bottom with a Linear Copper gradient.

42. Although copper is a good standard for metalwork, most stereo connectors are more gold or silver in hue. Go Image > Adjustments > Hue/Saturation and change the Hue setting to 18, and the Saturation to 25.

43. Now deselect the Jack Section 1 content and create a new layer, called 'Jack Section 2' between the Background and Jack Section 1 layers.

44. Select the Rounded Rectangle tool again and, using the same settings, draw a small button shape in the new layer, so that it protrudes from behind Jack Section 1.

45. Repeat the process used for filling and coloring Jack Section 1 on Jack Section 2. Deselect the new section after you've finished the coloring.

46. For added realism, highlights can be added using the Dodge and Burn tools. Let's use the Burn tool first, with the following settings for a Soft Round brush:

47. On the Jack Section 2 layer, apply the Burn tool to the area where the layer passes beneath Jack Section 1. This gives the appearance of a slight drop shadow:

48. Let's now use the Dodge tool to add some highlights. In the options bar, set the following attributes, once again with a Soft Round brush:

49. On both Jack Section 1 and Jack Section 2, apply the Dodge tool to the areas where the gradient gives the appearance of reflection. Don't apply the Dodge too liberally; subtle highlights will do.

50. When you are happy with the cable and jack, merge all the layers together except the background and rename the layer as 'Stereo Cable'.

Here's the cable after a few more highlights were added with the Dodge tool. I've also added a simple Drop Shadow to add to the realism:

Save the image as a PSD file somewhere on your computer with the layers intact so you may use the cable on other images or in other designs. The process was long and at times tedious, but some of the coolest effects, especially in realistic objects, require a bit of repetition. Here endeth the lesson.

2: Advanced circuit boards

Math has never been a favorite subject of mine. It's not that I find it difficult… it's more tedious than anything. However, I love the math behind Photoshop. Moving a mouse, selecting commands and warping pixels are all results of formulae I could never hope to recreate on paper. Photoshop makes math fun to a guy like me, and I don't have to count my fingers and remove my shoes to get the desired results.

1. Create a new image using the 640 x 480 preset with the Resolution set to 72 dpi.

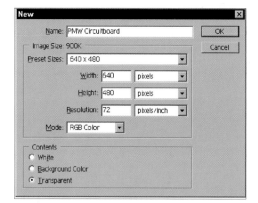

2. Click CTRL/CMD+SHIFT+N to create a new layer. Name this layer 'Board'. Select the Rectangular Marquee tool, and draw a large selection over the layer, taking up nearly the entire image, but leaving some space for a border.

3. Click on the foreground color square in the toolbox to open the Color Picker, and choose the color with the R, G and B values all set to 90.

4. Once you've set the color, click ALT+DELETE to fill the selection with the foreground color. We'll now add two filters that will result in creating a very subtle checkerboard effect.

5. With the newly filled area still selected, go to Filter > Noise > Add Noise. Create a Monochromatic Gaussian Blur with the Amount set to 15%.

6. Click OK to confirm the noise. We'll now add another filter, the Mosaic filter. Go to Filter > Pixelate > Mosaic and enter a Cell Size of 25 square.

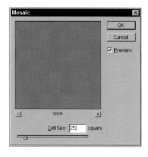

Although faint, there is now a checker box pattern on the layer that Photoshop recognizes, although the eye may have a difficult time perceiving it. This is the foundation for the circuits.

7. Go to Filter > Stylize > Find Edges. You'll be left with a faint grid pattern.

8. To further separate the pattern tones, go to Image > Adjustments > Brightness/Contrast. Increase the Contrast to 90 and click OK.

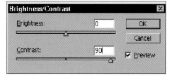

9. We'll now add some glowing edges (Filter > Stylize > Glowing Edges). Enter the following settings in the Glowing Edges dialog box:

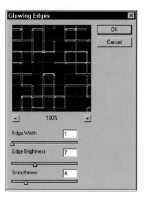

Here's where we're at so far, with our new glowing edges:

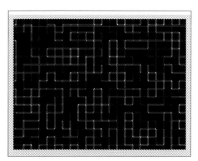

10. There is a nice pattern developing, but it can be enhanced even more. Again, go to Filter > Stylize > Find Edges, and then apply the Glowing Edges filter again. This time enter the following settings in the Glowing Edges dialog box:

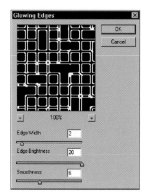

11. I find that inverting the image so that the circuits are black and the open areas white make the circuits easier to work with. Maybe this is just a quirk of mine, but it works. Go to Image > Adjustments > Invert (CTRL/CMD+I).

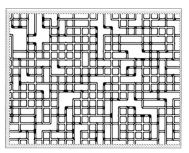

12. The circuits must now be separated from the white background. Go to Select > Color Range. In the Color Range dialog box, click the eyedropper on any black portion of the image. You may do this either in the dialog box or on the image itself. When selected, click OK.

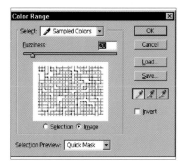

13. You should now have just the black areas – the grid – selected, copy the content to a new layer Layer > New >Layer via Copy (CTRL/CMD+J).

14. Now, select the Board layer in the Layers palette. We're going to add some Layer Styles to this area, so CTRL/CMD-click the Board layer to load it as a selection. Click the 'Add a Layer Style' icon and create a Bevel and Emboss using the following settings:

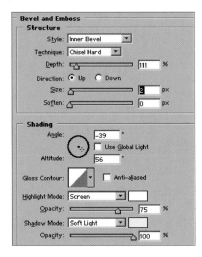

The effect of this bevel is quite subtle; so don't worry if you don't notice a huge difference.

15. Click on the words 'Gradient Overlay' on the left side of the dialog box, don't use the checkbox to choose this option, as this will just apply the default settings, but here we want to change the gradient color. You can do this by clicking in the Gradient window, to open the Gradient Editor. Click on the gradient stop on the right-hand side to change the color to green.

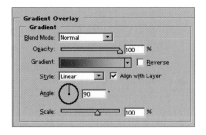

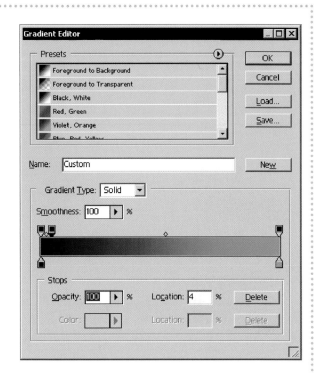

16. Finally add a default 'Inner Shadow' to the board; we will now merge these styles into one layer to apply them permanently. Create a new layer beneath the Board layer. Select the Board layer and go to Layer > Merge Down (CTRL/CMD+E) to merge it with the new layer. Rename the merged layer as 'Board'.

17. Now move on to Layer 1. First change its name to 'Circuits'. We are going to add some Layer Styles here too, in order to make the grid appear more three-dimensional. Click the 'Add a Layer Style' icon to add a Drop Shadow and enter the following settings:

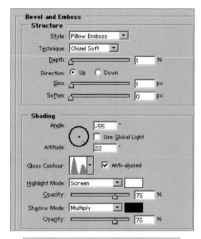

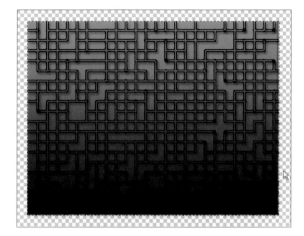

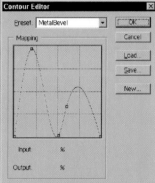

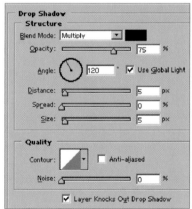

Notice the Layer Knocks Out Drop Shadow box. This is checked by default and it ensures that the drop shadow will show through partially transparent areas of the layer, rather than just at its edge.

Still in the Layer Style dialog, select Gradient Overlay from the left-hand menu. Enter the following settings:

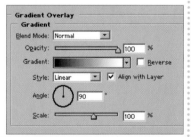

18. We'll also apply an emboss effect to this layer, so select Bevel and Emboss from the left-hand menu. Enter the following settings for the emboss. Set the Gloss Contour by clicking on the box to open the Contour Editor. Try and match the one shown in the screenshot.

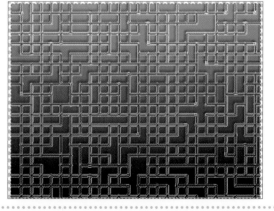

19. Click OK to confirm the Layer Styles. We'll now merge the Circuits layer using the technique we used previously. Create a new layer below Circuits, and then, with the Circuits layer selected, use the Merge Down technique. Rename the new merged layer as 'Circuits'.

20. Still in the Layers palette, select the Board layer. We'll apply a noise filter to this layer now. Go to Filter > Noise > Add Noise and enter the following settings:

21. Click OK to apply the filter. Take a look at the image below to check your progress.

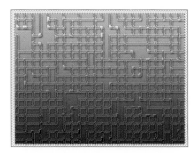

22. Continue by creating a new layer at the top of the Layers palette. We'll now use the Rectangular Marquee tool to create chips to affix to the circuit board. Enter the following settings for the tool in the Options bar:

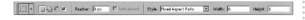

23. Make a selection about one inch square in the upper left quadrant of the layer.

24. Ensure that black is set as your foreground color and click ALT-DELETE to fill the selection with black. Keep the Marquee tool selected, but change the 'Style' setting in the option bar back to 'Normal.' Increase the zoom on the image, as this can be delicate work. Create a small rectangular selection as seen in the screenshot below and hit the DELETE key:

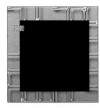

25. Move the selection down, leaving a black area between the deleted area and the new selection placement, and hit DELETE again. Continue around down the left side and then down the right side of the square, moving and deleting equidistant spaces. When done your image should look like this:

26. Now add a Bevel and Emboss using the following settings:

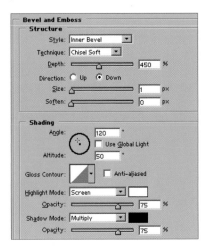

27. Still in the Layer Style dialog, select Drop Shadow. Enter the following settings:

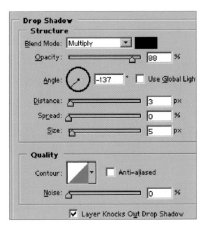

28. Click OK to apply the style settings. Your Black Thing should now look like this:

29. Return to the Rectangular Marquee tool and create a selection covering most of the face of the Black Thing.

30. Create a new layer above the layer you're currently on. Use the Gradient tool with the following settings to draw a White to Black gradient from upper left to lower right of the selection.

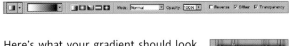

Here's what your gradient should look like:

31. Soften the effect slightly by lowering the Opacity of the gradient layer to 50%.

32. Click CTRL/CMD+D to clear the selection and use the Type tool to apply any text you like to the face of the chip.

33. Use Layer > Merge Down (CTRL/CMD+E) to merge the text layer with the gradient layer.

34. Now create a further layer beneath Layer 1. Select Layer 1 and then merge it with the empty layer using the Merge Down technique to apply the style permanently. Rename the newly merged layer as 'Black Thing 1'.

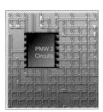

35. Duplicate the Black Thing 1 layer four times by dragging it onto the 'Create a new layer' icon. Select the Move tool and, one layer at a time, position the new Black Things around the face of the circuit board.

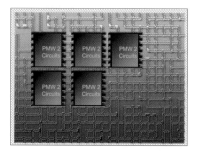

36. Not all components need to be the same size. Select one of the Black Thing copies in the Layers palette and click CTRL/CMD+T to enter Free Transform mode. In the options bar, change the width of the object to 60%.

37. Select the reduced Black Thing and duplicate that layer twice. Move these into place alongside the original copy.

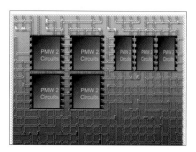

38. Once you are happy with the size and number of chips, select the topmost in the layer stack. Use Layer > Merge Down (CTRL/CMD+E) repeatedly until all the Black Thing layers are merged into one. Rename the merged layer as 'Black Things'.

39. We're going to make some glass diode-type objects now. Create a new layer at the top of the layer stack. In the toolbox, select the Elliptical Marquee tool and set the following options for this tool in the options bar:

40. Draw a circular selection on the new layer away from the Black Things.

41. Now go to Edit > Fill and select the setting here before clicking OK.

42. Open the Styles palette (Window > Styles). Load any glossy button/text style sets you may have available. For this example I'm simply using those I've created over the course of the last few chapters. You can find these on the CD.

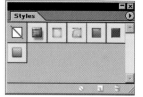

43. Deselect the circular selection that you should currently have. Now click on a Style to apply it to the gray circle. This gives the effect of having a lamp, a diode, or some other electronic thingamajig affixed to the circuit board.

44. Next, duplicate the layer several times, moving each object to a new position on the circuit board with the Move tool. Try applying different styles to the copies. When you have several in place, select the topmost glossy object and merge down until all the lamps are on a single layer. Rename the merged layer 'Knobby Things'.

As a rule, circuit boards are slotted on one side. Trust me, I've had a bit of experience yanking cards out of my stable of PCs. You can tell how much I've learned in the process by the highly technical names I've given the layers in this tutorial. OK, only kidding.

45. Select the Circuits layer in the Layers palette. Merge this layer down into the Board layer. The new layer will automatically assume the name of the bottom-merge layer, in this case Board.

46. Select the Rectangular Marquee tool and use the technique we used earlier on the Black Things to create slots at the bottom of the board. You need to make the rectangular selection, press DELETE, and then move the selection to the next slot area and repeat the process. Do this two or three times.

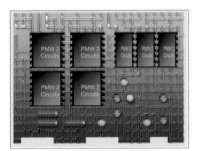

As an added extra, I've made a few resistor-type shapes using the Rounded Rectangle tool with a smooth Inner Bevel and a blue Color Overlay.

Take a look at that! A person not so familiar with the insides of a computer might mistake it for the real thing.

Let's take a look at the board from another perspective.

47. First, merge all layers except the Background layer together.

48. Duplicate the Board layer by dragging it to the 'Create a new layer' icon. Turn off the visibility on the original Board layer, by clicking the small eye next to it in the palette, and select the Board copy layer.

65

49. Let's now flip the copy around. Go to Edit > Transform > Flip Vertical.

50. Next, use Edit > Transform > Perspective to change the Height setting to 50%. Select the top left or top right Transform point and move it toward the center an inch or so.

Here's what my image looks like at this point:

51. As we have changed the perspective of the board, there should be an edge facing us. Duplicate the Board copy layer and then use the Move tool and arrow keys to move the new layer up two clicks.

52. Duplicate the layer you just moved, and again move it up two clicks with the arrow keys. Do this four times until you are satisfied with the thickness of the leading edge on the circuit board.

53. Select the topmost copy and then use the Merge Down technique until all the circuit board layers are merged together.

If you were to stack two or three of these circuit boards together as though they were attached to the inner workings of a PC, you would want to apply a Drop Shadow to help the effect. For the last example, I've applied a Drop Shadow, changed the perspective a bit on the duplicates and added a new background.

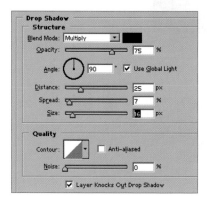

In this chapter, we have gone beyond the familiar simple wires, instead we've created a cable with realistic dimensions and features, thus increasing the complexity but also the authenticity of the object. It's the same with the circuits: rather than simply creating a pattern (for which there are a dozen applications, and not all electronic in nature), we took that several steps further to generate an actual circuit board.

Photoshop is a great tool and a fantastic program, but in reality it is only as good as the person using it. I hope that, above all else, you'll walk away with a hundred ideas on how you may apply these techniques to your own method of design.

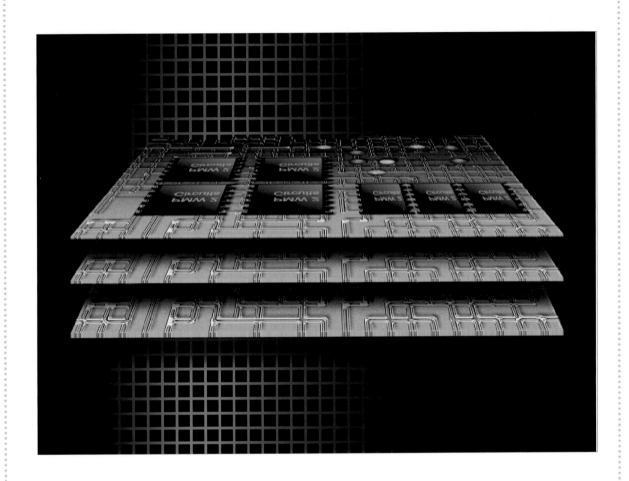

Chapter 5
Pattern generation

This chapter deals specifically with randomness, or at least the appearance of randomness. In fact, this chapter celebrates that aspect of Photoshop design.

I'll tell you right up front; there will be a lot of repetition of steps throughout the tutorials in this chapter, as well as from one tutorial to the next. The reason for this is that we'll be starting with something simple and then building on that until, by the final tutorial, we'll have some pretty fantastic effects. This chapter is a personal favorite of mine - I hope you enjoy it.

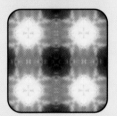

1: Basic masking patterns

1. Open the image `A1-Wood2.jpg` found on the CD.

> If you would like to add the pattern creation Actions to your arsenal, now would be a great time to start recording the Action. For information on recording Actions, please see **Chapter 8**.

2. Go to Image > Image Size.. The reason for the change in dimension is that most (most, not all) seamless patterns are square. In the Image Size dialog box, change the dimensions for the photo to those shown in the screenshot below. Make sure you start with 'resolution':

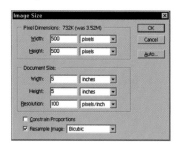

3. Click OK. Duplicate the Background layer in the Layers palette by dragging it to the 'Create a new layer' icon.

4. Go to Edit > Transform > Flip Horizontal.

Masking now comes into play. By using layer masks and gradients, Photoshop allows you to render portions of layers invisible and visible.

5. With the Background copy layer selected in the Layers palette, click the 'Add layer mask' icon on the bottom of the Layers palette.

> When you create a layer mask, the foreground and background colors reset to black and white, as these are the colors that will dictate which portions of the layer are revealed and which are hidden. Remember, when working with masks, black conceals and white reveals. When you select a layer without a mask, then the colors will revert to their original settings

6. Select the Gradient tool. In the options bar, apply the following settings to the Gradient:

7. Starting on the left edge of the image, draw the gradient straight across to the right edge of the image (using the SHIFT key to keep the line straight). This will render the right side of the layer visible, and gradually become invisible so that portions of both layers may be seen with the gray/blended portion of the gradient allowing both layers to blend in the center.

The screenshot below shows what the gradient will look like applied to the mask in the Layers palette:

8. Hit CMD/CTRL+E to merge the layers together.

9. In the Layers palette, duplicate the Background layer again.

10. Go to Edit > Transform > Flip Vertical.

11. In the Layers palette, click the 'Add layer mask' icon.

12. Select the Gradient tool. Starting at the top edge of the image, draw the gradient down vertically to the bottom edge of the image.

13. Hit CMD/CTRL+E to merge the layers together.

The image is seamless now, but prior to saving this as a reusable pattern, you may want to reduce the size of the image.

14. Go to Image > Image Size and enter the following settings in the Image Size dialog box and click OK:

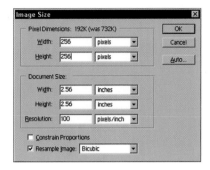

15. Reducing the size may decrease the resolution a bit, so go to Filter > Sharpen > Sharpen.

16. The pattern is ready to define and use. Go to Edit > Define Pattern. In the dialog box that appears, name the pattern.

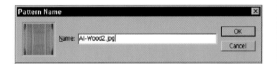

17. Click OK. The pattern is now loaded and ready to apply.

18. Let's give the pattern a test run to see if it is, indeed, seamless. Without closing the pattern image (we will return to it shortly), create a new image with the following attributes:

19. Go to Edit > Fill. In the Fill dialog box, select Pattern for the fill type and choose the new pattern from the loaded set. It will be in the last position. When it is selected, click OK to close the Fill dialog box.

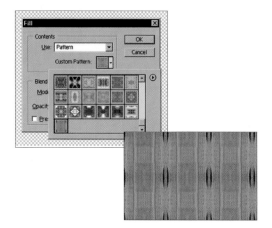

As you can see, the new image is filled with a nice, repeating wood pattern with no visible seams; each repetition of the pattern melds with the next without any stark lines where they meet. Minimize this image and return to the pattern image.

As it stands, the pattern is seamless top to bottom, and left to right. If we stretch the process out a bit further, the image can be made to match on all four sides equally.

21. Duplicate the Background layer of the pattern image. With the Background copy layer selected, go to Edit > Transform > Rotate 90° CW.

22. On the bottom of the Layers palette, click the 'Add layer mask' icon.

23. With the Layer Mask active, select the Gradient tool. Starting in the upper left-hand corner, draw the gradient down to the lower right-hand corner using the SHIFT key to constrain the angle to 45°.

24. Hit CMD/CTRL+E to merge the layers.

25. Again, duplicate the Background layer. Go to Edit > Transform > Flip Horizontal.

26. Click the 'Add layer mask' icon. Select the Gradient tool. This time draw the gradient across the image, from left to right horizontally.

27. Hit CMD/CTRL+E to merge the layers.

28. One more round of masking to go! Again, duplicate the background layer.

29. Go to Edit > Transform > Flip Vertical.

30. Click the 'Add layer mask' icon.

31. Select the Gradient tool. In the options bar, check the Reverse box. This is a very important step - it swaps the colors of the gradient, changing the portion revealed and the portion hidden, primarily for variation in the effect. Not checking this box will render a totally different result!

32. Starting at the top of the image, draw the gradient down to the bottom of the image. See the difference in the two images below:

33. Hit Cᴍᴅ/Cᴛʀʟ+E to merge the layers together. You may define this pattern now. When you fill an image with the pattern, you will have a unique tile pattern that resembles wood in tone only.

2: Pattern creation - sharper gradients

In the previous tutorial, the default, gradual black to white gradient was used throughout for an even blending of the layers across the majority of the image. By adjusting the gradient stops - narrowing the gap between them - more distinction can be pulled from the resulting pattern. Did I lose you? No problem this will explain what I mean.

1. To begin, open Al-Clouds3.jpg, found on the CD.

2. Duplicate the Background layer. Go to Edit > Transform > Flip Horizontal.

3. On the bottom of the Layers palette click the 'Add layer mask' icon.

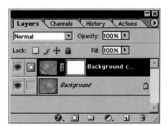

4. Select the Gradient tool. In the Gradient options bar, click on the Gradient window to open the Gradient Editor.

5. The loaded gradient is displayed in the editor. Click the first color stop on the bottom left of the Gradient Editor. Change the color to white (if it isn't already). In turn, select the Color stop on the right side and make sure it is set to black.

6. By moving the color stops closer together, we reduce the amount of blending between the layers making a starker transition. Click on the white color stop and enter 48% for the location. Click the black color stop and enter 52%.

7. Click OK to exit the Gradient Editor. In the options bar, set the following:

8. Draw the gradient across the image, starting on the left-hand side to the right-hand side (using the SHIFT key to keep the line straight).

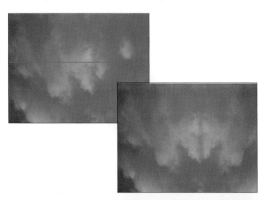

9. With the Background copy layer active, hit CMD/CTRL+E to merge the layers.

10. The image I used for this tutorial was taken straight from my digital camera without any adjustments made. Go to Image > Adjustments > Auto Contrast (CMD/CTRL+ALT+SHIFT+L). This will brighten the image, toning down the heavy blue shading and enhance the yellows in the clouds.

11. Now simply perform the steps seen in the previous tutorial for generating seamless patterns.

12. Go to Image > Adjustments > Brightness/Contrast. In the Brightness/Contrast dialog box increase the Contrast to +55 and click OK.

13. Save the pattern again. Now when you use the pattern to fill an image, you will have something close to the pattern shown below.

3: Patterns from beyond

Even though the previous tutorials resulted in some odd effects, we have barely touched the surface where pattern generation is concerned. This tutorial adds a few filters and distortions to the photo, taking the pattern generating to new heights.

> *I strongly recommend that you record this as an Action (see Chapter 8), since the end result never turns out the same way twice!*

Before we begin, I should point out that this is an excellent way to recycle every image you have. That being said, if you get hooked you could literally fill up your hard drive with unique patterns.

To demonstrate, I'm using a photo of my kids that didn't turn out very well. The focus was off, and in most cases this photo would be unusable for much. When we stick a pattern creator on it, suddenly a whole new realm of uses for the photo becomes apparent.

1. To begin, open the image `Kids-1.jpg`, found on the CD.

> *If you would like to save this process as an Action, please start recording now.*

2. Go to Image > Image Size Enter the following settings in the Image Size dialog box and click OK:

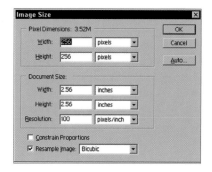

3. Hit CMD/CTRL+A to select the entire image.

4. To wipe out any border items that you may want to remove, we can apply a blur to it to clean it up. Go to Select > Modify > Border In the Border Selection dialog box, enter a width of 16 pixels and click OK.

5. Go to Filter > Blur > Gaussian Blur. Enter a blur radius of 12-14 and click OK.

6. Go to Select > Deselect (CMD/CTRL+D). Then duplicate the Background layer in the Layers palette.

7. Go to Image > Adjustments > Desaturate, and then Image > Adjustments > Invert (CMD/CTRL+I).

8. Go to Filter > Blur > Smart Blur. Enter the following settings in the Smart Blur dialog box and click OK:

9. Go to Image > Adjustments > Invert (CMD/CTRL+I).

10. Go to Select > Color Range. With the Eyedropper, select the white area of the image and click OK.

11. With the white selected, hit the DELETE key.

12. Go to Select > Deselect (CMD/CTRL+D).

Looks a bit messy now, but trust me, it gets better!

13. CMD/CTRL-click the Background copy layer in the Layers palette to load it as a selection.

14. In the Layers palette, create a new layer above the Background copy layer.

15. Click on the Foreground color in the Toolbox to open the Color Picker. Enter the following values and click OK:

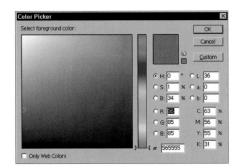

16. Go to Edit > Stroke. Enter the following settings in the Stroke dialog box and click OK:

17. Deselect (CMD/CTRL+D) and then set the layer Blending Mode to Overlay.

18. Go to Filter > Blur > Gaussian Blur. Enter a blur radius of 3 to 4 pixels and click OK.

19. Select the Background copy layer in the Layers palette. Change the Blending Mode to Soft Light.

20. Select Layer > Merge Visible (CMD/CTRL+SHIFT+E).

21. Now it's time to apply some Filter distortions. Go to Filter > Distort > Wave. Enter the following settings in the Wave dialog box and click OK:

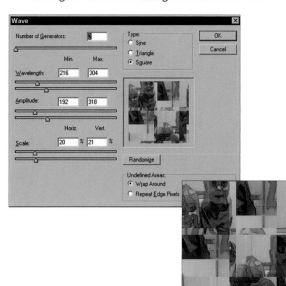

22. Duplicate the Background layer in the Layers palette.

23. Go to Image > Adjustments > Desaturate and then Image > Adjustments > Invert.

24. Go to Filter > Blur > Smart Blur. Enter the following settings in the Smart Blur dialog box and click OK:

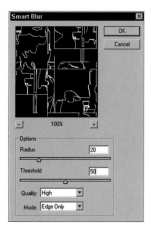

25. Go to Image > Adjustments > Invert again.

26. Go to Select > Color Range. In the Color Range dialog box, select white with the Eyedropper tool. Click OK.

27. With the white area selected, hit the DELETE key.

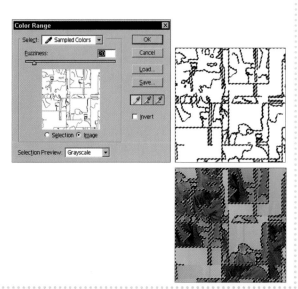

28. Deselect the area (CMD/CTRL+D). In the Layers palette, change the Blending Mode of the selected layer to Overlay.

29. Select Layer > Merge Visible. In the Layers palette, duplicate the Background layer.

30. Go to Filter > Artistic > Paint Daubs. Enter the following settings in the Paint Daubs dialog box and click OK:

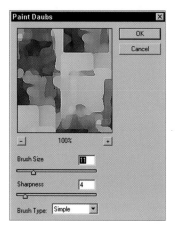

31. In the Layers palette, set the Blending Mode for the Background copy layer to Soft Light.

32. Select Layer > Merge Visible. In the Layers palette, duplicate the Background layer.

33. Go to Edit > Transform > Flip Vertical.

34. With the Background copy layer active, click the 'Add layer mask' icon on the bottom of the Layers palette.

35. Select the Gradient tool in the toolbox. In the options bar, set the following attributes for the gradient. Use the gradient settings from the previous tutorial, but make sure you select 'Reverse'.

36. Starting in the upper left-hand corner of the image and holding the SHIFT key, draw the gradient diagonally to the lower right-hand corner.

37. Select Layer > Merge Visible. In the Layers palette, duplicate the Background layer.

38. Go to Edit > Transform > Flip Vertical.

39. With the Background copy layer active, click the 'Add layer mask' icon on the bottom of the Layers palette.

40. Apply the gradient vertically, from bottom to top.

41. Select Layer > Merge Visible (SHIFT+CTRL/CMD+E). In the Layers palette, duplicate the Background layer.

42. Starting at the top of the image, draw the gradient straight down to the bottom of the image.

Below you can see the image so far:

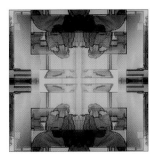

43. Select Layer > Merge Visible. Duplicate the Background layer in the Layers palette.

44. Go to Edit > Transform > Rotate 90° CW.

45. With the Background copy layer active, click the 'Add layer mask' icon on the bottom of the Layers palette.

46. Starting in the upper right corner of the image, draw the gradient to the lower left corner whilst holding the SHIFT key.

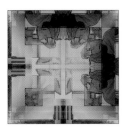

47. Select Layer > Merge Visible. In the Layers palette, duplicate the Background layer.

48. Go to Edit > Transform > Flip Vertical. And then Edit > Transform > Flip Horizontal.

49. With the Background copy layer active, click the 'Add layer mask' icon at the bottom of the Layers palette.

50. Starting in the upper right corner of the image, draw the gradient to the lower left corner again holding the SHIFT key.

51. Select Layer > Merge Visible.

The completed pattern is seen below. That's quite a difference from the original photograph! It's totally unrecognizable from the original children image.

52. You can now save the pattern, as it's totally seamless. Go to Edit > Define Pattern. Name the pattern and click OK. It will now be loaded into the available patterns for use in layer fills, Layer Styles and so forth.

You needn't take my word for it, the screenshot below shows a new image filled with the pattern just defined:

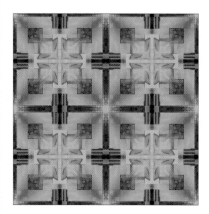

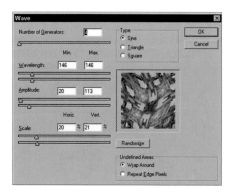

I've saved the steps as an action (I'll get to that shortly) and, using the pattern image we just created, re-ran the entire thing through the same process. The new pattern is seen below.

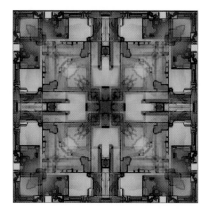

You may add further warping power by including another Wave command in the action. For example, I've inserted an additional Wave command just after the Paint Daubs command and the layer merge that followed.

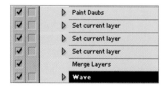

Now when the pattern is run through the action, an entirely new design is rendered as shown below:

Remember the Glass Sphere image we created in **Chapter 2**? What would happen if that image were run through the 'pattern warper'? Below you can see the before and after pictures.

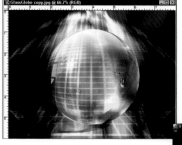

My favorite subjects for the 'pattern warper' actions I've created are images of people. The skin tones add a fantastic quality that is hard to duplicate with just a sunset or a tree. Below you can see an initial photograph prior to the pattern warp, and three variations of the effect:

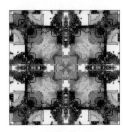

Keep in mind that all three patterns are of the same photograph.

We'll cover Actions in more detail elsewhere in the book and you'll find a bonus chapter all about Actions on the CD. For now, I'll quickly show you how to save the pattern generator.

1. Select the set in the Actions palette where your action is located.

Actions can only be saved as sets.

2. In the upper right corner of the Actions palette, click the small arrow to open the Actions Menu. Select **Save Actions** from the menu.

3. Find a spot on your computer to save the action set to. I have several folders on my computer for actions of all varieties. These need not be kept in the Photoshop directory; anywhere on your computer is fine.

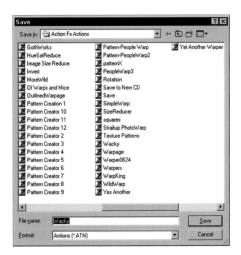

There you have it. Using combinations of masks, gradients and filters, the patterns you can generate from a single image are limitless. No need to throw away old photos, as these techniques offer new life to images that otherwise have little or no use.

Chapter 6

Magic and Monsters

Much time has been spent in the preceding chapters creating images either from scratch or by manipulating photographs until the end result is unidentifiable from the original image. This chapter retains the character of its subjects, in that the end result will resemble what could be a real creature, however fantastic.

1: Skull face

1. To begin, open the image `Andy-Face.psd` from the CD. Those of you who have read *Photoshop Most Wanted 1* will recognize this guy; in that title I turned him into a borg. This time I'm going to help him lose a little weight!

2. This effect merges two photos together; so open the second image, `SKULL-Front.psd`.

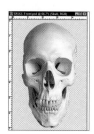

3. With the skull image active, ensure that the layer with the skull is active and then drag this layer into `Andy-face.psd`. A new layer will be generated to hold the skull just above the face layer. Now close `SKULL-Front.psd`.

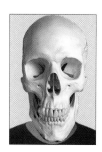

4. In the Layers palette, change the opacity of the Skull layer to 60%. This is required for the next step, as the skull needs to be resized to fit the shape of the face.

5. Hit Ctrl/Cmd+T or go to Edit > Transform > Scale. Moving the transform points in the center of the top, bottom and sides, reduce the size of the skull to match the head beneath. Some key points to watch are the teeth, the nose and eye sockets. For instance, the teeth should appear over the lips. One common mistake is placing the top of the skull at the top of the peak of the hair. The hair actually extends above the skull an inch or so.

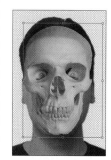

6. Click the check mark button in the options bar, or hit the Enter key, to accept the transformation. In the Layers palette, increase the opacity of the Skull layer to 100%.

7. Select the Face layer in the Layers palette and, with the mouse, drag it above the Skull layer.

In the past I've done this effect without using facial distortions such as Liquify, but I've found that increasing features such as the eyes really enhance the effect.

8. Go to Filter > Liquify. On the left-hand side of the Liquify dialog box you will see a series of tools, which are used to distort the brush area. The sixth from the top is the Bloat tool, which expands an area by moving pixels away from the center of the brush area. Select this tool now.

9. On the right-hand side of the Liquify dialog box, change the Brush size for the Bloat tool to 90. Leave all other settings where they are.

10. Starting with either the right or left eye, move the mouse so that the center of the eye is in the middle of the brush. Hold down mouse button until the eye swells.

11. Repeat the bloating process on the other eye. Try to keep the two eyes proportional to one another.

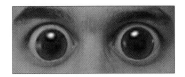

12. The next tool we'll use is the Warp tool. This is used to redraw an area of the image by pushing the pixels forward as you drag. Select the Warp tool now from the top of the Liquify toolbar (left-hand side of the dialog box).

13. On the right hand side of the Liquify dialog box, change the Brush size for the Warp tool to 15.

14. Push the area beneath the eyebrows up away from the eye without warping the eye itself.

Some bleeding may occur, which means that some of the color from one area may 'bleed' onto a differently colored area. For example in the right eye below. Don't worry about this now, we can, and will, correct that later.

15. Click OK to accept the Liquify distortions and to close the Liquify dialog box.

16. In the Toolbox select the Polygonal Lasso tool and set the following attributes in the options bar.

We need to have the 'Add to selection' button chosen, as we'll be making two areas, which we'll be treating as one selection. We'll add 8 pixels of feathering in order to round the corners of our selection as much as possible.

> Holding down the SHIFT key while making a selection automatically changes the setting to 'Add to selection'.

17. Make large circular selections around both eyes, including the areas above the eyes that were warped previously with the Liquify tool. Don't include the eyebrows in your selections. (We're using the Polygonal Lasso rather than an Elliptical Marquee so that the selection has an irregular shape).

18. The eyes need to be placed on their own layer. Go to Layer > New > Layer via Cut (CTRL/CMD+SHIFT+J). Once the eyes have been placed in their own layer, select the Face layer. Change the layer Blending Mode to Overlay, which means you'll see the shading of the skull image but the color will be blended with the skin tones of the Face layer.

19. We have reached the point where it would be prudent to have a background rather than work with a transparent layer. This will assist in seeing the edges of the skull and face so that they may be blended together. In the Layers palette, select Layer 1.

20. Go to Edit > Fill (or use the shortcut SHIFT+BACKSPACE to open the dialog box). Use the settings shown below for the fill.

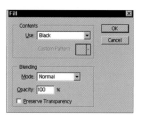 

Now there's a strange looking character! He looks terrified... must be looking in a mirror.

21. CTRL/CMD-click the Skull layer to load this layer as a selection.

22. Select the Face layer with the skull selection still active and then click the 'Add layer mask' icon on the bottom of the layers palette. As you can see in the screenshot below, this creates a mask over the face in the same shape as the skull.

23. Hit the D key to reset the default colors; black to foreground, white to background.

In the Toolbox, select the Brush tool. In the options bar, set the following attributes for the Soft Round brush:

The skin tone from the Face layer in Overlay mode has left a nasty stain on the teeth. This guy needs to hold back on the coffee!

24. In the mask attached to the Face layer, paint over the teeth with the black brush. This will mask the areas of the Face layer that stained the teeth. Adjust the brush size as needed to get in all the nooks and crannies.

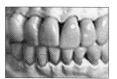

25. Staying with the same layer, select the face image rather than the mask, by clicking on the thumbnail of the face in the Layers palette.

26. At the moment, the hairline leaves a stark line across the skull's forehead. In the Toolbox, select the Smudge tool; use a Soft Round brush at around 35 pixels with Strength set to roughly 50%.

27. Use the Smudge tool to blend the hairline into the skull as seen here:

28. Next, select the eyes layer (Layer 3) in the Layers palette.

29. CTRL/CMD-click the eyes layer to generate a selection. Now, on the bottom of the Layers palette, click the 'Add layer mask' icon.

30. Now return to the Brush tool again. Set the following attributes in the options bar for a Soft Round brush:

31. Make sure that you have the mask selected and that black is set as the foreground color. Paint the areas above the eyes lightly to blend them with the mask.

32. With the Move tool, move the eyes up or around in the socket until you are happy with their position. They may not require movement at all; this is up to you.

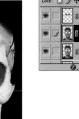

33. Duplicate the Face layer in the Layers palette. As the Face layer is in Overlay mode, doing this will increase the depth of color the face applies to the skull. You may also desire to increase the contrast of the eyes layer by making a Brightness/Contrast adjustment.

Now that's one happy Andy!

2: Do you believe in Fairies?

Perhaps elves are a figment of the imagination, and their derring-do is better left to Tolkien or other scribes of the fantastic. Or perhaps they really do exist and it's just a case of knowing where to look in order to find one! In this section we're going to build on the techniques used in the skull tutorial to create our very own elfish creatures.

First, a subject is required; for this example a human female will work nicely.

1. Open the image Woman-1.jpg, found on the CD.

2. With no further ado, go directly to Filter > Liquify.

3. From the tools on the left, select the Bloat tool. On the right side of the Liquify dialog box, set the Brush size to 110.

4. As we did before in the Skull face tutorial, center an eye in the middle of the Brush. Holding down the mouse, expand the eye until it's quite a bit larger than life.

5. Repeat the process for the other eye.

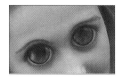

6. Select the Warp tool and set the Brush Size to 10.

7. With a lighter touch and smaller brush than used with the skull tutorial, raise the eyebrows of the subject so that they extend up and away from the eye. Repeat the process for the second eye. Try to keep them as uniform and straight as possible. This is a female elf, so think delicate!

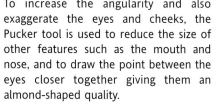

8. In the Liquify toolbox, select the Pucker tool, found just above the Bloat tool. Humans have soft faces, whereas elves tend toward sharper features. To increase the angularity and also exaggerate the eyes and cheeks, the Pucker tool is used to reduce the size of other features such as the mouth and nose, and to draw the point between the eyes closer together giving them an almond-shaped quality.

9. Alter the Brush size to 133.

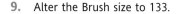

10. Set the brush above the bridge of the nose, right between her eyes. Hold down the mouse to shrink the area, drawing the eyes closer together without decreasing their size.

11. Now place the brush over the point of her nose, and again hold down the mouse button to shrink this feature.

12. Before reducing the size of the mouth, let's inflate the lower lip a bit. To reduce it now would make the lips too thin to be convincingly female. Select the Bloat tool again and center the mouse over the lower lip and inflate it a bit.

13. Now return to the Warp tool and move the lower cheek in closer to her mouth.

14. Reverting back to the Pucker tool, and with a Brush size of 255, center the brush over the model's lips and click/hold the mouse button to shrink the lips, jawline and chin.

15. Now decrease the Brush size of the Pucker tool to 90. Center her nose within the brush, and reduce it further.

16. Select the Warp tool. Again, center the tool over her nose, but this time move the nose up away from her upper lip and toward the eyes. This will give the model a pug quality. Click OK to accept the Liquify distortions.

17. Time to add a sparkle to this Queen of the Forest. Our aim is to create a duplicate of the image, which we'll turn into a negative, and then use the resulting white areas to create magical shimmers around our elf's face. Start by duplicating the Background layer in the Layers palette.

18. Before creating the negative we need to take all of the color out of the duplicated layer, so go to Image > Adjustments > Desaturate or use the shortcut CTRL/CMD+SHIFT+U. Then hit CTRL/CMD+I (Image > Adjustments > Invert) to invert the blacks and whites.

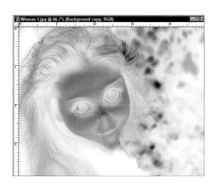

19. Let's apply a blur now. Go to Filter > Blur > Smart Blur and enter the following settings in the Smart Blur dialog box:

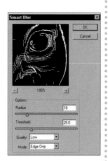

Here's the result of this blur, the white areas of the negative image now form a trace around the elf's face:

20. We now want to take all of the black out of this layer, so go to Select > Color Range. In the Color Range dialog box, click on a black spot in the image to select all black in the layer.

21. Hit the Delete key to wipe the black from the layer, and then deselect the layer (Select > Deselect or CTRL/CMD+D).

22. Let's now apply another blur, this time a Gaussian Blur (Filter > Blur > Gaussian Blur). Enter a blur radius of 8 pixels in the Gaussian Blur dialog box, and click OK.

23. Select the Eraser tool in the Toolbox and set the following attributes for a Soft Round brush eraser:

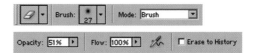

24. Use the tool to erase the white blur from above the eyes.

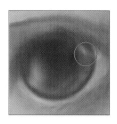

25. In the Layers palette, create a new layer above the white blur layer. Click on the foreground color in the toolbox and then find a bright tone for use on the eyes: I'm using a bright green.

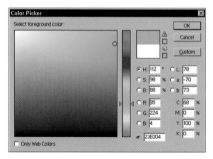

26. Select the Brush tool and change the Brush size to 20, leaving all other settings alone. They will have kept the settings from the previous use of the paintbrush.

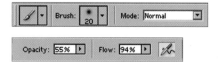

27. Paint around the eyes in the new layer to color them.

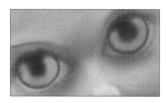

28. Set the foreground color back to black and change to a hard-edged brush. Use this to fill the pupil portion of the eyes with black, maintaining the rounded edge of the pupil.

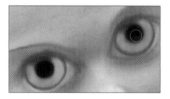

29. Now set the foreground color to white and reduce the Brush size to 9. Paint a single reflection on each eye. Reduce the size of the brush even further and paint two more on each eye. Finally, reduce the Brush size one more time and again spray a spot on each eye.

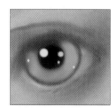

Here is the Elf Maiden thus far:

30. In the Layers palette, select the Background layer.

31. Select the Burn tool from the Toolbox and set the following attributes for the Burn tool in the options bar, before running the Burn tool lightly over the lips to darken them slightly.

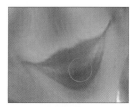

32. Now create a new layer just above the Background layer.

33. Select a bright red color for the foreground.

34. Return once again to the Brush tool. Change the size to 28, and lightly paint over the lips, especially the lower.

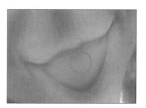

35. Back in the Layers palette, change the Blending Mode of the red paint layer to Soft Light.

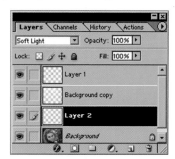

36. Next, select the Background layer again. Go to Image > Adjustments > Brightness/Contrast and increase the contrast of the Background layer to +20.

37. Go to Layer > Merge Visible (CTRL/CMD+SHIFT+E) to merge all the layers together into the Background layer.

38. We have a little clean-up to do around the eyes and lips where the Liquify tool has distorted and stretched the skin. Select the Clone Stamp tool for this job. In the options bar set the Brush size to 14.

39. Sample an undistorted area close to the spot needing correction by ALT-clicking the un-warped area. Then click the mouse over the area to be corrected, stamping the new skin into place.

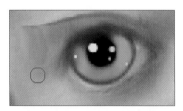

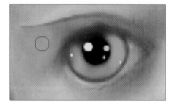

Here's the new Elf Maiden!

Every Elf Maiden needs an evil twin, and this girl is no exception. For variation (save the original first), go to Image > Adjustments > Hue/Saturation. Set the Hue slider to -100 and click OK.

How evil is that?!

Photoshop opens doors that previously only the imagination could open. Try these techniques on photos of friends and family; they may seem horrified at first, but soon they'll be hooked and want to see what else you can do!

Chapter 7
Type Madness

I mentioned in the first *Photoshop Most Wanted* book my addiction to type effects. That addiction remains firmly in place, though the reason for the attraction is still a mystery to me. The alphabet started as, and remains, my palette of choice when creating effects in Photoshop. Without further ado, here are a few of my experiments. Enjoy!

Rotten wood paneling

I'm sure you've seen wooden text effects before, but this tutorial will go beyond the norm to create some realistic looking rotten wood. While working through this tutorial, I recommend recording the steps as an action. For those who decide to give it a try, there are a couple of commands just for you. If you decide not to record the action, simply skip the step where noted. For more information on actions, please see Chapter 8.

1. To begin, create a new document of 900 x 600 pixels with a transparent background.

If you'd like to record this as an action, start recording the new action now.

2. On the bottom of the Layers palette, click the 'Create a new layer' icon.

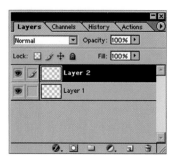

Action alert: *Recording stops, or messages, to yourself during the course of an action instructs the user on steps they need take in order for the action to proceed. As this action requires the user to enter text with the Type Mask tool, a stop is required. If a stop is not inserted at this point, the action will type the same text for you every time the action is played. By stopping the action and entering your own type, the text may be changed with the same end effect applied.*

If you're recording an action, stop recording now. Open the Actions menu and select **Insert Stop**. *Enter text in the 'Stop' dialog box similar to the following: "Please enter your text using the TYPE MASK TOOL (found under the regular Type tool in the Toolbox). This usually works best with a thick font set to 160-200 points".*
Ensure that Allow Continue is unchecked at the bottom of the 'Record Stop' dialog box, and click **OK**.

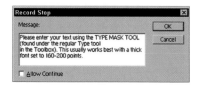

Once the Stop is entered, click the Record button on the bottom of the Actions palette once again.

3. If you're not recording this as an action, make sure that you have entered some text using the Type Mask tool (found under the regular Type tool in the Toolbox). Use a thick font set to 160-200 points.

4. As we're working with wood, it's time to select some wood tones for our color swatches. Click on the Foreground color in the toolbox. Enter a color value of H=44 S=37 and B=89.

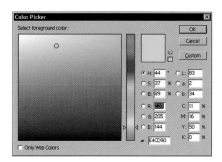

5. Now click on the Background color. Enter a color value of H=41 S= 99 and B= 58.

6. Select the Gradient tool in the toolbox and choose a foreground to background Linear gradient:

7. Starting at the top of the type selection and holding the SHIFT key, draw the gradient straight down to the bottom of the type selection.

8. Go to the Channels palette, (Windows > Channels if it is not open already). Click the 'Create new channel' icon at the bottom. A new channel named Alpha 1 will appear.

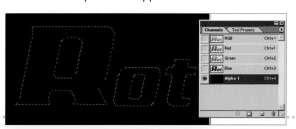

9. Go to Edit > Fill > White, with 100% opacity and click OK.

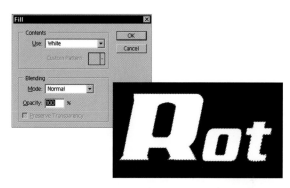

10. The Crystallize filter will help create the pattern to generate the rot area of the wood. This will be run three times, clicking OK after each time to apply the selection. Go to Filter > Pixelate > Crystallize. Do this three times, with the Cell Size set to 32, then 14 and finally 9.

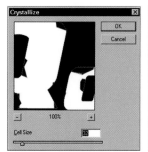
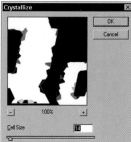
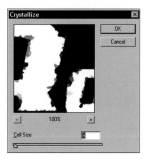

11. Deselect the text area (CTRL/CMD+D) and then CTRL/CMD-click the Alpha 1 channel. The white and light gray areas will be selected, but the darker grays will not, leaving a jagged edge selection as shown below:

12. With the jagged selection active, return to the Layers palette and select Layer 2. Go to Layer > New > Layer via Copy (CTRL/CMD+J). If you turn off the visibility of all but the new layer, then you can see the effect of the crystallization.

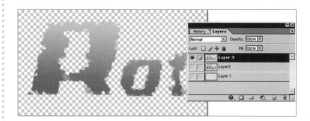

13. The following steps will apply some basic wood grain to the new layer. Go to Filter > Noise > Add Noise, and add a Monochromatic Gaussian Blur at 25%.

14. Go to Filter > Blur > Motion Blur. Set the Angle to 90° and the Distance to 24 pixels.

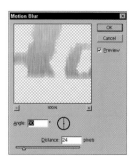

15. Let's draw some detail out of the grain with the Brightness/Contrast command. Go to Image > Adjustments > Brightness/Contrast. Edge the Brightness down to about –9, and move the Contrast up to +33.

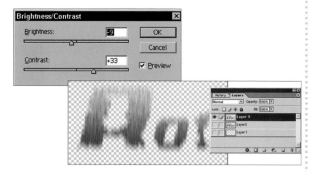

16. Click the 'Add a layer style' icon on the bottom of the Layers palette. Select Bevel and Emboss from the style menu. Enter the following settings for the bevel:

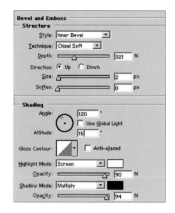

Here's my image so far, with all layers visible. The bevel has pulled the wood grain away from the background text, giving the appearance of three dimensions. We can now start applying texture to the base text to further enhance the effect.

17. In the Layers palette, select the original text layer, Layer 2. Go to Filter > Noise > Add Noise. Use the same settings as before but set the Amount to around 12.65%.

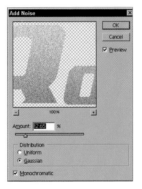

18. Click the 'Add a layer style' icon at the bottom of the Layers palette. Select Drop Shadow from the menu. Enter the following Drop Shadow settings:

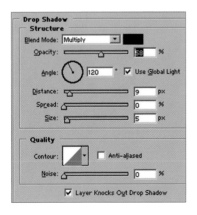

19. Select Bevel and Emboss from the list on the left hand side of the Layer Style dialog box. Enter a bevel with the following settings:

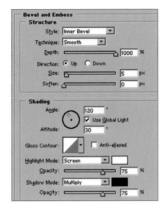

20. To separate the color of the lower layer from the paneling layer further, click CTRL/CMD+U to open the Hue/Saturation dialog. Decrease the Hue to -11 and click OK.

21. CTRL/CMD-click Layer 2 in the Layers palette to activate a selection of the layer's contents.

22. Open the Layer Style settings for Layer 2 again. Select Inner Glow and enter the following settings:

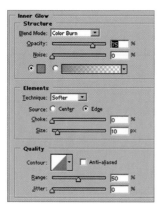

23. Select Bevel and Emboss from the left-hand menu on the Layer Styles palette. Enter the following bevel settings:

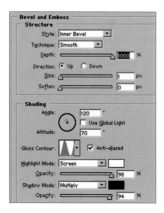

24. Select Stroke from the left-hand menu on the Layer Styles palette. Enter the following 'Stroke' settings:

25. Deselect the type (CTRL/CMD+D) to check the progress.

Although I had to close the Layer Styles for Layer 2, we're not through with them yet.

26. Open the Layer Styles for Layer 2 again. In the left-hand menu, select Texture beneath the 'Bevel and Emboss' settings.

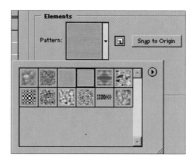

27. Click on the Pattern window. Load the default pattern set and select the pattern named Wood. Set the Texture settings to the following:

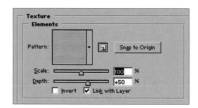

The screenshot below shows the image thus far. By applying a texture to the bevel settings, the pattern from the picture draws out wood grain in Layer 2 moving horizontally, rather than vertically as in Layer 3. The effect is that of a wood veneer having been peeled away from the base paneling.

28. Select Layer 3 in the Layers palette. CTRL/CMD-click Layer 3 to generate the jagged selection seen below.

29. Click the 'Create a new layer' icon on the bottom of the Layers palette.

30. Change the foreground and background colors to dark tan/light tan respectively.

31. Go to Edit > Stroke. Enter the following settings in the 'Stroke' dialog box:

32. Set the Blending Mode of the Strokes layer to Color Burn, 100% opacity. The screenshot below shows the Blending Options for Layer 4 as seen from within the 'Layer Styles' dialog box:

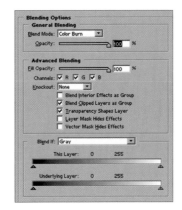

33. Use CTRL/CMD+D to deselect.

The stroke and Blending Mode change applied to Layer 4 darkens the edge of the foreground paneling, as shown below.

34. Select Layer 3 in the Layers palette.

35. Let's work on the bevel just a bit more. Open the Layer Style settings for Layer 3, and select Bevel and Emboss. Enter the following settings:

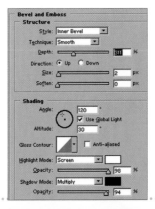

36. Select Color Overlay from the left-hand menu. Enter the following settings:

37. The brown you should use is shown below:

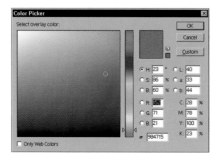

38. Lastly, select Stroke from the left-hand menu. Enter the following settings:

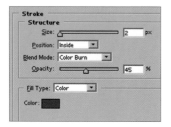

The images below show the completed text with and without backgrounds.

I love the realism of this effect! It reminds me of the worn-out desks in my old school. Remember those? Names from the past 50 years etched in the surface, and gum just as old affixed to the bottom. Ah, sweet memories...

Stone and embedded glass – two effects in one

As I write this, Colin is sitting in my office as we develop the joint projects that appear later in the book. The discussion arose about standard type effect tutorials. I read these tutorials for inspiration and to see where the trends are going, to study the steps other authors and teachers take to reaching their end effect.

I enjoy reading these tutorials, but I have a problem with some of them. Don't get me wrong, they're very good at getting the reader from start to finish in the quickest manner possible. But the fact of the matter is some of the richer effects require more steps.

All that was to preface the length of this tutorial. There are a lot of things going on, but to reach the end result, the extended steps are needed. What I'd like you, the reader, to focus on, is the process for generating more in-depth effects. A bit more time spent on a project, even something as seemingly unimportant as type, can make the difference between a ho-hum cool effect and a mind-blowing trend setter that will produce imitators and adoring fans far and wide.

1. To begin, open Al Background 3.jpg found on the CD.

2. Click CTRL/CMD+N to create a new layer.

3. Select the Type Mask tool. In the options bar, set the attributes for your font. For this tutorial, I'm using a very large font size so that you can see the effects clearly. The font I've used, HorstCaps, can be downloaded for free from www.fontmagic.com/cate/old8.html. The font settings are:

4. Type on the new layer. When you first enter the text, the ruby colored mask will be active; click the check mark on the right-hand side of the options bar to activate the type selection.

5. Hit D to reset the foreground and background swatches. Black will be in the foreground and white in the background.

6. Hit ALT+BACKSPACE to fill the selection with the foreground color.

We're now going to add a white stroke to the lettering, which we'll then offset from the black text to create a subtle 3D effect.

7. Hit the X key to exchange the foreground and background color swatches. This will automatically set the Color in the 'Stroke' dialog box to white.

8. Create a new layer, and with this layer selected go to Edit > Stroke. Set the following attributes in the 'Stroke' dialog box.

9. Select the text layer and use the Move tool (V) to move the selection with the arrow keys a few clicks to the left and a few clicks up. The black text selection is now slightly to the right and slightly higher than the white stroke.

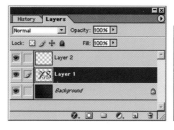

10. Make sure you have the stroke layer selected and then hit DELETE to clear the white left in the selection.

11. CTRL/CMD-click the stroke layer to generate a selection around the remaining white.

12. Go to Filter > Noise > Add Noise. Enter the following settings in the 'Add Noise' dialog box:

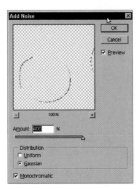

13. In the Layers palette, CTRL/CMD-click Layer 1 to generate the type selection again, but keep Layer 2 as the active layer.

14. Go to Filter > Blur >Motion Blur. Set the angle of the blur to 0 degrees and the distance to 25 pixels. Click OK.

15. Use CTRL/CMD+D to deselect. In the Layers palette, select Layer 1.

16. Click the 'Add a layer style' icon on the bottom of the Layers palette. From the menu select Bevel and Emboss. Enter the following settings for the bevel in the Styles dialog box and click OK:

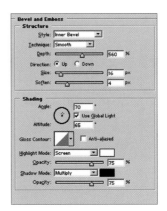

17. Duplicate Layer 2 twice in the Layers palette. Select the topmost duplicate layer and hit CTRL/CMD+E twice to merge the duplicates back into Layer 2. This will further increase the brightness of the white highlight being created.

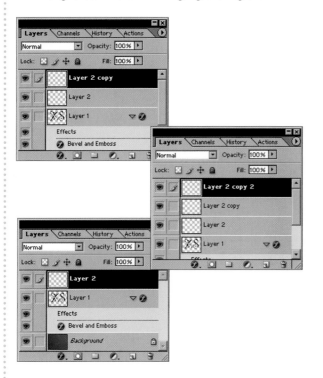

18. If it's not active, go to Select > Reselect to activate the selection with layer 2 active in the Layers palette.

19. Go to Filter > Blur > Gaussian Blur. Enter a blur radius of 6 to 7 pixels and click OK.

20. Click the 'Add a layer style' icon on the bottom of the Layers palette. From the menu select Bevel and Emboss. Enter the following settings for the bevel in the 'Styles' dialog box:

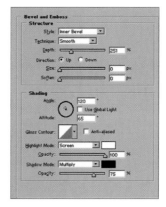

The text will now have a nice glossy appearance, but with half the highlighting in a separate layer. This may seem like the long way to do things (why not just apply all the highlights with a layer style, you may ask), but the effect will pay off later.

21. Use CTRL/CMD+SHIFT+I to invert the selection.

22. Go to Select > Feather. Enter a feather radius of 2 pixels.

23. Hit the DELETE key twice. This will clean up any stark white edge on Layer 2.

24. Use CTRL/CMD+D to deselect.

25. Select Layer 1 in the Layers palette. CTRL/CMD-click Layer 1 to generate a selection of the type layer again, without the feather applied in the previous step.

26. In the toolbar, set the foreground color to the following red. Click OK.

27. Fill the selection in Layer 1 with the foreground color.

28. Click D to set your foreground color to black and then select Gradient Overlay from the menu on the left of the 'Styles' dialog box. Enter the following gradient settings for a foreground to transparent gradient:

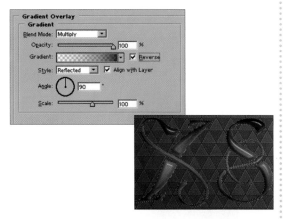

29. In the Layer palette, select Layer 2.

30. Go to Image > Adjustments > Hue/Saturation. Enter the following settings in the 'Hue/Saturation' dialog box:

> In order to enter a Hue value of 259, you'll need to check the Colorize box first.

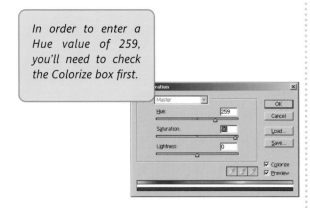

31. Hit CTRL/CMD+D to deselect.

32. Select Layer 1 in the Layers palette. Click the 'Create a new layer' icon on the bottom of the Layers palette.

33. Go to Edit > Fill. Enter the following settings in the 'Fill' dialog box:

34. Go to Filter > Render > Difference Clouds.

35. Apply the Difference Clouds four more times by hitting CTRL/CMD+F four times to reapply the filter.

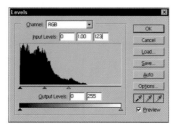

36. Go to Image > Adjustments > Levels. Move the right and center sliders toward the left to increase the contrast between the white and black areas of the difference clouds.

37. Hit CTRL/CMD+I to invert the color.

38. In the Layers palette, set the layer Blending Mode to Overlay, with an opacity of 100%.

39. The text is taking on a glassy feel now, but we can enhance this by giving it the illusion of transparency and depth. We'll do this by selecting Layer 1 once again, and opening the Layer Styles. Select Bevel and Emboss again. We entered settings previously: I'll now show you how adjusting these settings can change the type from solid plastic to transparent plastic or glass. Once 'Bevel and Emboss' is open, enter the following settings:

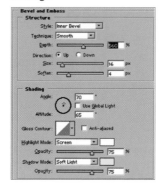

40. Select Inner Shadow from the left-hand menu of the 'Styles' dialog box. Enter the following settings:

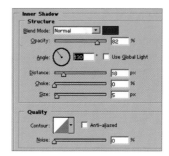

41. CTRL/CMD+D to deselect.

In the finished effect you should be able to distinguish several distinct effects: clouds, transparencies, warped surface and so forth. As you can see, combining effects can enrich even the simplest of designs.

107

Chapter 8

Layer Styles and Actions for Cool Effects

At the top of my list of the absolute coolest features in Adobe Photoshop is the ability to save presets, tools and techniques for later use and distribution. Actions and automation are my original passion, but from those little scripts I've branched out into layer styles, brushes, and virtually any setting that can be saved.

I could write an entire book on the subject of automation and presets, and perhaps I will do so down the road. In the meantime, I hope this section will at least give a hint to why styles and actions are so popular, as well as some instruction on making and distributing your own cool effects.

Layer styles - A quick run through

So what are layer styles exactly? Layer styles are settings that can be applied to layers and saved as a group of presets for use later. This allows for easy creation of identical effects used across multiple web pages, photos and so forth. They really are as simple as that. Any style may be saved for later use, and any saved style may be altered to suit your particular needs and design tastes. Like Actions, Curves and other customized settings, layer styles can also be distributed to other Photoshop users for their work.

1. When you first open the Layer Styles palette (Window > Styles), several default layer styles are already loaded.

These are Adobe's little gift to you; they are, however, of limited use. If you were to use one of these in your work, every other person in the world with Photoshop would instantly recognize them and deride you for it. They will help me illustrate the application of styles here though.

2. Open an image to use as a background (anything will do – you could use A1_Background2.jpg found in the Chapter_02 folder on the CD). With white as the foreground color, select the Horizontal Type tool. With a large font, type some text in a new layer.

3. Clicking another layer style icon in the same set: the settings are changed to those of the second style applied.

As you can see, this is easy stuff and even basic styles can produce cool results.

Layer Style palette viewing options

Before we go into the process of building layer styles, let's take a look at the palette itself and a few menu features available.

The viewing modes for the palette are changed by accessing the Layer Styles menu. This is opened by clicking the small arrow in the upper-right portion of the Layers palette.

By default, the Layer Styles palette is in Small Thumbnail mode when opened initially. This mode is great if you don't care to see the name of the style or the effect, as it displays the style examples as very small icons with no name associated.

But you may wish to see more information about the available styles. Let's check out some other views. Select Text Only from the Layer Styles menu.

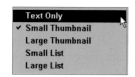

This view allows you to see the Layer Style names with no examples. When the designer created the Layer Styles for the default set, they were gracious enough to include in the file name what the style was designed for: buttons, images, textures, or text. This is a good rule of thumb for your own styles, and will help you keep track of what the original intent of the style was for, what image type it works best with, and so forth.

The obvious drawback to this mode is that you have no example to choose from, as in one of the Thumbnail modes.

While we're here you may as well take a look at the other modes: Large Thumbnail, Small List, and Large List. It's really up to you which mode you prefer to use in future.

You can also manage the Layer Style sets and views via the Preset Manager.

If you have loaded other Layer Style sets and would like to return to the original default set supplied by Adobe, selecting **Reset Styles** from the Layer Style menu will remove the loaded styles and replace them with the set we looked at previously.

On the bottom of the Layer Styles menu are several other sets you may load by selecting them from the menu. Those seen in the example screenshot below are sets also included with Adobe Photoshop. If you save other sets to the Layer Styles directory in Photoshop, these will appear here also. There is a limit to how many will appear. If you are in the habit of collecting and saving styles, this author recommends saving them outside of Photoshop entirely. They may be loaded from anywhere on your computer or a CD, and it's best not to clutter the Photoshop folders any more than is necessary.

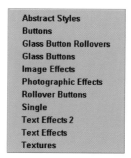

To load additional sets that you've saved to your computer, select Load Styles from the menu. You may then point Photoshop to the place that the additional styles are saved, select a single set, and click Load.

If you select Load Styles, the new set will be added to those already resident in the Layer Styles palette.

If you want to replace a loaded set entirely with a new set, select Replace Styles from the Layer Style menu. Again, Photoshop will ask you to locate the layer style set. Find it, load it, and the new set will be the only one appearing in the Layer Styles palette. You may then click on a style to apply it to the layer contents.

For some of the more advanced users, these may be old hat. For the new users or those just becoming familiar with Layer Styles, don't let them intimidate you. For quick, easy and slick effects, there is nothing faster than these little goodies.

1: Creating a layer style

As you've seen, loading and applying layer styles is extremely simple. The process of creating and editing them is a bit more in-depth, but this is only due to the wide variety of choices you have in creating the style. I'll walk you through the process of creating a layer style for text, but please keep in mind that I only have space to scratch the surface of the settings available to you.

1. To begin creating the style, open a background image. In order to achieve a similar effect to the one I have created here it would be a good idea to use a red background. Create a new layer and enter some type as we did in the previous example.

2. At the bottom of the Layers palette, there are a series of icons that through the course of the book you should have become familiar with. The first icon on the left-hand side gives you style options to apply to your layer. A menu will open with several selections.

3. Open the menu and select Bevel and Emboss...

> *When you select something from the Layer Styles menu, the 'Layer Style' dialog box appears. The one downfall about the 'Layer Style' dialog box is that it's so large it covers the image that you're working on. For this reason, Adobe has included a layer style preview on the right-hand side. You may gauge your progress by looking at this preview, or moving the 'Layer Styles' dialog box to the left or right so you can see your image.*

Since we selected Bevel and Emboss... from the menu, the default bevel settings appear. As you proceed in adding styles to the layer, they're applied to both the image and the preview. You must click OK for them to be accepted, however.

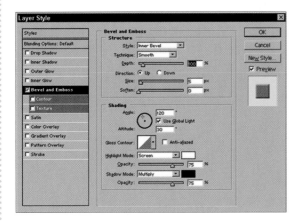

Increasing the depth of the bevel to 1000% changes the image and the example accordingly.

4. Let's make a style, starting by changing the 'Bevel and Emboss' settings. Enter the following settings for the bevel in the 'Layer Style' dialog box:

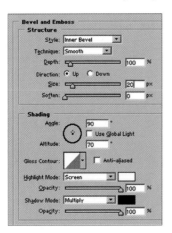

5. On the left-hand side of the 'Layer Style' dialog box, select Inner Shadow.

6. Enter the following settings for the Inner Shadow:

7. Take a look at the image, noting the progression of effects thus far. You'll notice that the settings we've applied have given the white text a glossy bevel, with the inner shadow creating the illusion of depth; sort of like clear plastic.

8. Select Drop Shadow from the left-hand menu. Enter the following drop shadow settings:

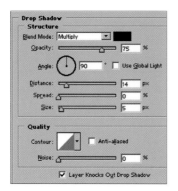

9. Select Outer Glow from the menu. Change the color to an orange hue.

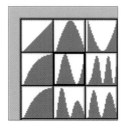

10. Changing the contour of the glow to Ring alters the glow effect to a neon-style outline.

11. Changing the contour to Ring Double intensifies the effect, dividing the glow into two halos.

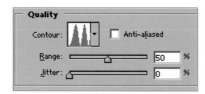

12. Select Inner Glow from the left-hand menu. Enter the following settings for the inner glow using an orange hue again:

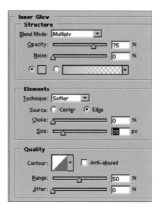

13. Change the Size to 24px and the Contour to Ring - Double.

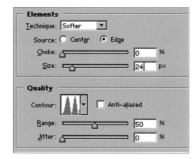

As you can see, we now have a double ring surrounding the type and a pair of orange stripes within the text also. This may not appear useful, but the exercise is to teach you how to add the settings together.

14. Select Contour from the left-hand menu. Change the default contour to Cove - Deep. This levels out the center of the bevel, driving it to the edge of the type.

114

> Increasing the sharpness and number of peaks in the contour adds further depth to the effect, as when the Sawtooth 1 contour is applied.

15. For this example, let's stick to something not quite so intense. Change the contour to Ring.

16. The Satin setting applies a sheen to the text. This is not really a color overlay, but more a highlight. Select Satin from the left-hand menu and enter the following settings using a blue color:

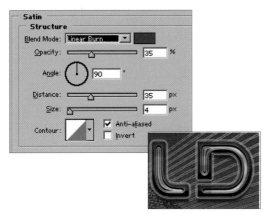

17. Select Color Overlay from the left-hand menu. Enter the following settings for the color overlay using an orange hue:

18. Now select Gradient Overlay from the left-hand menu. Enter the following settings for the gradient overlay in the 'Layer Style' dialog box (the gradient I've used is Steel Blue found under the Metals presets):

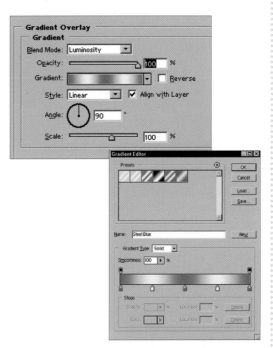

19. Take a look at the text to gauge the progress.

20. Drop the opacity of the gradient overlay to 60%. This way, when we apply a pattern overlay, the pattern will be visible behind the gradient.

21. Go to Pattern Overlay. Select the Optical Checkerboard pattern in the default patterns set.

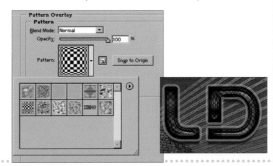

115

22. Finally, select Stroke from the left-hand menu. Enter the following Stroke settings using a red hue:

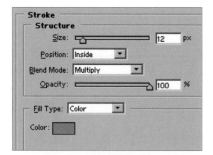

23. Hey, what happened? The stroke made the background appear through the text! Actually the answer is pretty simple. Since the background is primarily red and the stroke is set to multiply the red color used in the stroke, the background becomes visible due to the closeness in hue between the background and the stroke. We will change that later, but I quite like the translucent effect, so let's save the layer style as it is now for later use.

2: Saving a layer style

1. Click the New Style button on the right-hand side of the 'Layer Styles' dialog box.

2. A dialog box will open asking you to name the style before you save it. Once you've named it (or allowed Photoshop to assign the next sequential name), click OK. Naming is part of the process, and you should choose a name that best reflects the effect and what it is to be applied to. For instance 'Red Plastic Bevel-TYPE' might work well for this style.

> That's it – you've saved the layer style you just created. It now appears in the loaded set as the last icon on the bottom right.

In the Layers palette, the styles applied to the layer appear as an expanded menu. The small arrow to the right of the layer name will expand or collapse the menu. The 'f' tells you a layer style has been applied to the layer.

3: Editing layer styles

Editing a pre-made layer style is as simple as changing the settings. That's all there is to it. When I want to add a few quick styles to my arsenal, often I'll load a set I've saved previously and apply one of the styles to some text. Then with a few quick alterations, I clear the set from the palette, save the new style by itself, alter that style, and save the alterations several more times until I have 12 new styles or so and save the new set.

1. Let's alter the style we just created to make a few more custom styles. Open the Bevel and Emboss settings for the Layer Style. Enter the following settings for the bevel in the 'Layer Style' dialog box using a light blue/purple hue for the shadow color:

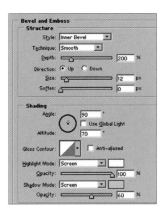

2. In the left-hand menu, uncheck the Contour option.

3. Select Outer Glow from the left-hand menu. Enter the following settings for the outer glow using a pink color and a Ring contour:

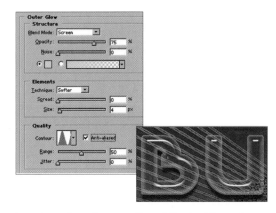

4. Just those few changes altered the text to a glossy, seemingly transparent plastic. The shadow is a bit dark for a transparent object though. Select Drop Shadow from the left-hand menu. Enter the following drop shadow settings in the 'Layer Style' dialog box:

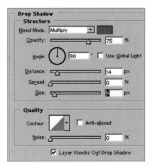

5. Select Pattern Overlay from the left-hand menu. Enter the following settings for the pattern overlay:

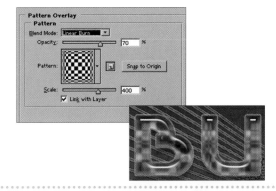

6. I'm going to show you a couple of cool little options available with the stroke style settings. Select Stroke from the left-hand menu. Enter the following stroke settings using an orange color:

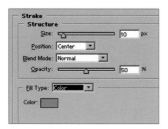

7. With the stroke option, you're not restricted to a color stroke only. You may also stroke the layer with a gradient or a pattern. Click the small arrow next to Fill Type and select Gradient from the menu.

8. When Gradient is selected, a few gradient options appear. Open these options and select Shape Burst from the gradient style menu.

9. Using a standard black to white gradient, the shape burst option applies the gradient as a bordered outline, as seen below:

10. Reduce the size of the gradient stroke to 7px, and change the position to Outside.

11. This is a cool little trick for beveling the layer on the edges only. Select Bevel and Emboss from the left-hand menu. Open the Style menu. On the bottom of the style menu is a selection called Stroke Emboss. When this is selected, the bevel will only be applied to the stroked area. If you increase or decrease the size of the stroke, the bevel increases or decreases to match it.

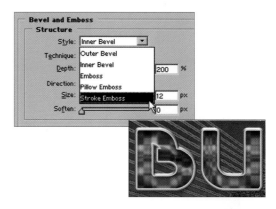

12. For this example, I'll return to the standard Inner Bevel and save the layer style. Once again click on the New Style... button and name the layer style appropriately.

13. The new style again appears at the bottom of the Layer Styles palette.

14. Once you have several styles and would like to save them permanently, open the Layer Styles menu and select Save Styles… from the menu. Create a folder on your computer to store them, or find one already in place. Name the style set, and click Save.

The image below shows the new style as applied to the layer.

It's always good to test the style against a second background, so in the image below I've added a layer of black behind the text layer.

Once saved, the style can be applied to any shape on any layer or image you choose with a simple mouse click.

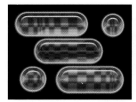

Actions – a quick run through

This is it. These little scripts are what started the whole Photoshop ball rolling for me, and still hold a place of esteem in my heart. I've branched out considerably since finding Actions, but always return to them like old friends. The original intent of Actions was for quick batch processing of multiple photos, but some designers realized this was an extremely narrow view, as most of the commands in Photoshop can be recorded and replayed, making them an excellent tool for streamlining website or artistic design.

Still, there remains very little information on the Internet about creating and saving Actions. Most books only give them a cursory glance, if mentioning them at all. I do have more tutorials on the subject on my website, so if you find them intriguing I encourage you to visit once you've made it through this section of the book (http://actionfx.com).

Let's take a look at the Actions palette, and hopefully I'll be able to shed some light on its operation and usefulness.

First, you may access the Actions palette by going to Window > Actions. You may also bring it to the fore by hitting F9. Once the palette is visible, it appears with several Actions available. In the example below there are several Actions I've created residing in the palette.

In the previous image, the palette is in **Edit**, or **List** mode. It has been called both, but I prefer Edit mode as this view is required to change or record actions. We'll play with this mode more in a bit. In the example above, the sets containing actions are displayed. To access the actions themselves, the arrow next to the set name needs to be clicked. This expands the set, showing the actions contained therein. **Actions may only be saved in sets.** For instance, an action must be placed in a set in order for the Save Actions command to become available. Also, the set must be highlighted. An action set may contain one action or many, but even a single action must be in a set.

You set up the action options from the Actions menu, which is accessed by clicking the small arrow in the upper right corner of the Actions palette.

The second mode of the Actions palette is Button Mode. When the palette is in this state, the actions cannot be edited; the action will simply run to completion when clicked.

In Button Mode, the actions appear as simplified buttons. The actions in the loaded sets are displayed, and not the sets as in Edit Mode. If an action was assigned a color code during creation, then the button will be the color assigned to it. Also, if any shortcut key combinations (up to 60 available) were assigned, these will appear alongside the action name.

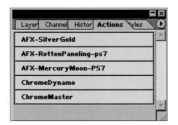

To load actions, open the Actions menu and select Load Actions… from the list. Find the actions in the folder you saved them to, select the action set and click Load.

Once loaded, you can select the action by clicking on the action name. Now when you click the 'Play selection' icon at the bottom of the palette or click the action button in button mode, the action will start running. It will replay the settings used when it was recorded exactly as the designer of the action set them.

Sometimes additional steps that aren't recordable need to be performed, or special instructions need to be followed for the action to work properly. In these instances you may see a pop-up message (called a **Stop**) appear giving instruction on steps to take before proceeding.

In the case of this action, I've done as the Stop requested and entered some text using the Type Mask tool set to a large font size. Once done, I hit the 'Play selection' icon again to continue the action.

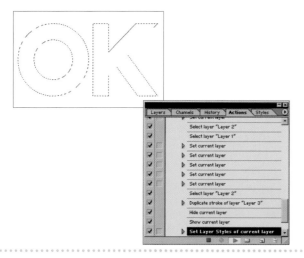

A Stop may also appear at the end of the action. The designer often places one here to say, "Thank you", offer contact information and so forth.

Once done, if no errors were received, the action should have run through to completion, leaving the same effect the action's creator saw when the action was first recorded.

You may edit commands in an action by finding the command in the action and double-clicking it. If the command has a dialog box attributed to it, it will appear and the action will start recording. You can enter the new setting, click OK, and the action will record the new setting and stop recording for you.

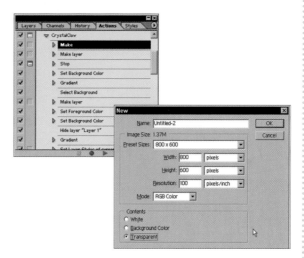

Sometimes changing action settings will affect the performance of the action, giving error messages and stopping the action. For instance, I've changed the Make setting at the top of the action's command list to use a transparent background rather than the white it was initially filled with. When the action is re-run with the new setting, an error pops up when a Select Background command is reached. Why? Because the action was to select pixels from the background, and now none are present.

This is not always debilitating; often you may just click Continue and the action will proceed normally. On other occasions, a totally different effect is reached at the end of the action, as is the case here.

Changing the Make command back to the original settings restores the action when replayed.

Actions may also run on different sized objects and selections, depending on how they were recorded. For instance, the action example below requires a type selection again. The font size of some of the text can be reduced or enlarged, and the action will still run normally.

4: Creating Actions

As stated previously, actions can only be saved as sets. Many actions can be saved to a set, or just a single action; however you do it, a set must be present. Let's walk through the process of creating an action.

1. To begin, ensure the Actions palette is in Edit mode. If not, change it in the actions menu by clicking Button Mode to uncheck it.

2. On the bottom of the Actions palette, click the 'Create new set' icon. If you do not, the new action will be placed in the existing action set (or active set if more than one are loaded). We want the new action to be saved by itself for the purposes of this tutorial, so creating a new set and placing the new action there will allow us to do this. If a new set is not created now, it may be created later and the action moved there then. This icon looks like a file folder.

3. Name the set, or just click OK. You can change the name later.

4. A new, empty Action set will appear in the Actions palette at the bottom of the loaded actions list.

5. Next to the 'Create new set' icon is the 'Create new action' icon. Click this with the set selected to create a new action within the set. You can either name the action in the dialog box or name it later.

6. Shortcut key combinations can be assigned to the action when you create it initially. Using combinations of the F (function) keys, the SHIFT key and CTRL/CMD, up to 60 shortcut key combinations can be assigned to different actions.

7. The actions you create may also be color-coded to categorize them for photos, text, buttons, or whatever categories you care to create. For this example I'll be creating a text action, and coding it blue. When in Button Mode, the button for this action will have the assigned color.

8. Clicking Record in the 'New Action' dialog box starts the recording process. Unless you stop it at some point, all the commands you apply to the image from here on will be recorded into the action. The depressed red icon on the bottom of the Actions palette indicates the action is recording.

9. For the first command, I'll record the creation of a new image. This is done normally, just as though the action were not recording.

10. Once you've clicked OK in the 'New' dialog box, the command appears as the first function in the recorded action, complete with all the settings assigned to it.

11. Now to proceed with the image creation. First I'll fill the background with a gradient.

12. Next I'll enter some text with the Horizontal Type Mask tool.

13. For the next step, I'll copy the selection to a new layer.

14. To make the type stand out from the background, I'll apply a layer style.

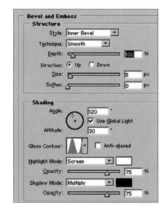

15. Now I'll stop the action by hitting the 'Stop playing/recording' icon on the bottom of the Actions palette.

16. Replaying the action gives me the exact same result as when I recorded the action, including the same font and same text.

17. Running the action again, I can stop the action at the point where the text is entered, by hitting the stop icon, the escape key etc, and change it to my own message and my own font by highlighting the selected type with the Type tool selected.

18. When the action completes its run, the new font is in place with the same bevel settings applied to the original file. Running the action and changing the font again reveals a similar result.

19. Once the action is complete to the designer's tastes, double-clicking the Action Set name allows you to rename the set. Click OK to accept the name change.

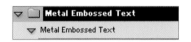

If you're saving a single action to a set, generally you'll just rename the action with the same name as the set it's contained in.

20. To save the action, select the set in the Actions palette.

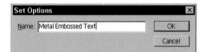

21. Go to the Actions menu and select Save Actions… from the menu. Find the folder on your computer where you would like to save the action to, and click Save.

When you change the mode of the palette, the action will be resident at the bottom of the list, complete with the color-coding assigned to it before.

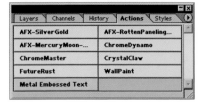

5: Using Actions as tutorials

The single most prevalent question I receive via my website is, "How did you do that?" referring to a particular technique or action result from something they downloaded from my web page. The action plays just fine, but watching and memorizing the steps to duplicate it without the action can be a bit tricky.

You could change the **Playback Options** by clicking on this choice in the Actions menu. This will allow you to set the speed at which an action will play through, in order to allow you to absorb the processes the action plays through with a short interval between each step.

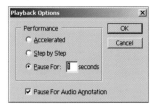

The drawback with this solution is that you cannot see the exact settings in the action. Clicking commands in the action to see the settings applied works for those with dialog boxes, but what about the settings that don't have dialog boxes?

There is a trick you can pull that lets you use action files as step-by-step tutorials, ready for printing with each step clearly defined and ready to be studied, copied and learned. An action is basically a text file that Photoshop assigns an .atn extension to, allowing it to recognize the file as a macro to be followed. You can, however, save any action you want to learn from as a text file, viewable in Notepad, a Word document or whatever text editor you have that will allow you to view documents with a .txt extension.

As an example, I've loaded an action I created a while back.

When played, the action creates a multi-layered metal effect that I think looks pretty cool. What if I want to duplicate the effect as a tutorial for use in an online article? I can't quite remember how I did it, and the action is very long; memorizing the process would be extremely time-consuming.

To save the action as a text file, first all other actions need to be deleted from the palette. If not, then all commands for all actions will be saved in the text file, and that could take up a couple of reams of paper if printed!

Make sure you have saved the actions, as shown in step 21 above, before you delete them. Then you can simply drag and drop them into the trashcan icon at the bottom of the Actions palette, safe in the knowledge that you will be able to access these actions later by going to **Load Actions** in the Actions menu.

1. To save the action as a text file, highlight the action set in the Actions palette and hold down the CTRL/CMD key and the ALT key. Open the Actions menu and go to Save Actions… You'll notice that when the Save dialog box appears Actions (*.TXT) appears in the Format slot on the bottom. Enter a name for the action text file, as this does not carry over from the Action you're saving.

2. Find the folder you'd like to save the text file to and click Save.

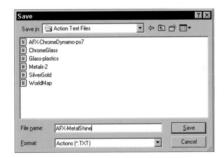

3. Open Notepad or another text editor. Find the file you just saved and load it into the text editor.

You may now print the file and use it as a visual guide or tutorial to walk you through the process of recreating the effect! Now there are no secrets between you and action designers across the globe.

Distributing Actions and Layer Styles

Once you have saved an action or layer style set to your hard drive, anyone with Photoshop 7 should be able to use it on their system. It is a simple matter of sending them the file, which they can then load into Photoshop and apply to their own images and text. The Adobe Exchange is an excellent site allowing people to redistribute their creations to the masses.

Adobe Exchange:
http://share.studio.adobe.com/Default.asp

That's it for the layer styles and actions chapter. I hope I've been able to shed a little light on these powerful tools, and helped you on the way to creating your own customized effects.

Chapter 9

From Clip Art to 3D

What is 3D really? A 2-dimensional object has height and width; the third dimension is depth. While we can't truly create depth in Photoshop or any other flat medium, we can create the illusion of the third dimension. In this chapter and the next, we'll look at how to become a magician and create the illusion of depth using the tools in Photoshop.

To create the illusion of depth there are three big players:

- **Lighting**. Where light hits an object and reveals surface density and convex surfaces.
- **Shadows.** Where light is obstructed and reveals depth by the density of the shadows and shows concave recesses.
- **Perspective**. Where the appearance of an object's size diminishes over distance.

You'll see these principles come into play over the course of the next few tutorials. To stay with the spirit of Most Wanted, let's jump right into it!

Transforming clip art images

This tutorial will change the way you use clip art. Clip art can sometimes be flat and boring, lacking in any depth or realism (of course there is some clip art that is excellent and fine just the way it is). I'm going to show you how to take the simple drawing on the left and transform it into the image on the right. Best of all, you will need no artistic abilities at all to do this.

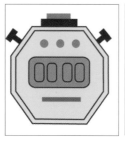

1: Importing a vector object to Photoshop

As you may already be aware, vector objects are those based on mathematical anchor points. For example, there may be an x point here and a y point there, and there's an instruction to draw a radius of a circle using the two, or to join them with a straight line. Certain stroke widths and colors may be assigned to them. These objects aren't based on any particular size and therefore they're resolution-independent.

Photoshop on the other hand mainly uses raster images. These are based on actual pixels. A pixel is a tiny point that may be filled with any color. All your photos are a combination of tiny pixels that appear as smooth objects.

A lot of clip art comes in vector form. The main formats are EPS (Encapsulated Postscript) and AI (Adobe Illustrator). When we place these objects into Photoshop they are **rasterized** or, in English, converted from vector to raster (Math to pixels).

There are several ways of bringing clip art into Photoshop. For this book we'll use the following method; this is the simplest and most flexible way to do it.

1. Create a new document called Clip art, sized 800 x 600 pixels, with the resolution set to 72 ppi for screen or 300 ppi for print.

Once you've created the new document, you'll want to import the clip art. Go to File > Place and browse to the file called ClipArt.pdf in the Chapter_09 folder on the CD. (Don't worry about creating a new layer – the object will come in on its own layer).

2. Your clip art will appear in your document with a box around it. The box indicates that it's still in vector format.

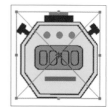

3. Drag on one of the corner points while holding down the SHIFT key to resize the object. It's very important to resize the image now; because once you convert it to a raster you'll lose quality by resizing. Remember that a vector object can be scaled without loss.

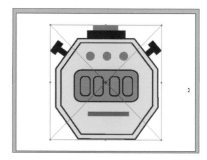

4. Press the Enter key to apply the transformation and the image will become rasterized. The image is now on its own layer and is a raster (or bitmap) object.

The next step is to separate all the elements of the image onto separate layers.

If you're familiar with vector programs such as Illustrator, Freehand and CorelDraw, separate the layers in the vector program and import all the layers separately into Photoshop. If you do this, you can skip the next few steps.

2: Separating the layers

1. Select the first object using the Magic Wand tool. In this case we're selecting the buttons on the stopwatch. To select more than one object at a time hold down the SHIFT key and click with the Magic Wand tool. Keep the tolerance at the default 30.

2. Go to Layer > New > Layer via Copy (CTRL/CMD+J) to copy the selection to a new layer. You'll now see the buttons on their own layer. Don't forget to name the layers for ease later on.

3. Continue copying the elements of the original object layer in the same fashion until each part is on a new layer. Your Layers palette should look something like this now:

4. Select the main section of the stopwatch and hide all the other layers.

5. Let's use the layer styles to add some depth to this. Click on the 'Add a layer style' icon at the bottom of the Layers palette to add a layer style. Apply an inner bevel as shown. Pay special attention to the Gloss contour, this gives us the shine on the bevels.

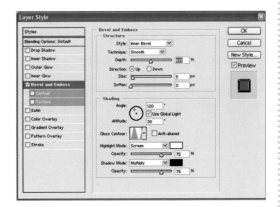

Your main body should look something like this now:

6. Show the button layer now.

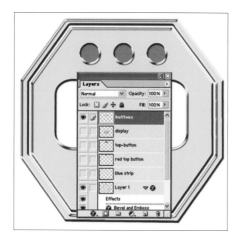

7. Apply a bevel as the layer style for the buttons, using the settings shown here:

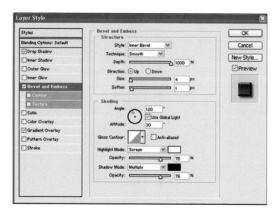

8. Also apply a gradient overlay using the copper gradient and Multiply mode to remove the copper color. We want to use the texture from the copper gradient, but not the color. Apply a default drop shadow as well.

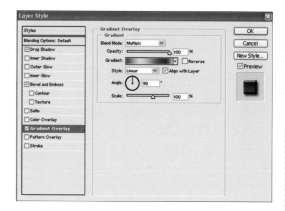

They're looking much better already.

The best way to add depth to cylindrical objects is with the use of gradients. We're now going to use three totally different approaches to apply gradients to shapes.

9. Reveal the top section of the watch. Ctrl/Cmd-click the layer thumbnail to load a selection around the shape. We're going to use an adjustment layer this time so that the selection will make sure the adjustment is applied to the selected area only and not the entire image.

10. Click on the 'Create a new fill or adjustment layer' icon in the layer palette. The adjustment layer options will pop up. Choose Gradient.

11. Enter the Gradient Fill settings as shown:

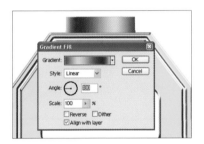

12. Change the Blending Mode to Luminosity to remove the color. This is a really quick way to apply a gradient. Later in this tutorial we will create a new gradient. This way you will be able to choose which method you prefer.

13. Now reveal the top part of the button. We are going to do exactly the same thing, but we'll use a different method to help build your skill set.

14. Add a gradient overlay layer style by opening the 'Layer Style' dialog as above. Choose the same gradient (copper) and the Luminosity Blending Mode.

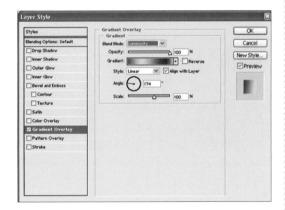

Here we've achieved the same result as above, just using a different way to achieve it.

Now for the third method: we'll apply a gradient to the push buttons.

15. Reveal the push button layer.

16. Since both the buttons are the same, it will be quicker to apply the effect to one button and then duplicate it. Draw a selection around the second button using the Rectangular Marquee tool. Press DELETE to delete it.

17. We should just have one push button remaining. CTRL/CMD-click on the thumbnail to select the object.

18. Click the Gradient tool to bring up the gradient options in the options bar. Now double-click inside the Gradient window to open the Gradient Editor, and make a custom gradient as shown. To add a color, just click below the gradient bar and a point will appear. Double-click the color picker to define the color of the point.

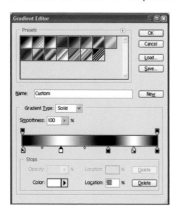

19. Set the gradient options to a Linear Gradient, then click and drag with the Gradient tool at the same angle as the button, but only go across the width of the shaft of the push button, as shown, to constrain the gradient to the shaft itself.

20. You should now have a metal-looking gradient across the push button shaft. Do not deselect yet.

21. Now to keep the selection only on the top part of the button. Choose the Polygonal Lasso tool.

22. Choose Subtract from selection from the options bar. Click around the shaft, to remove the selection from that area.

Just the top part should be selected now.

23. Apply the same gradient in exactly the same manner, except this time, drag the width of the tip of the push button instead of the narrower shaft.

The push button is looking a lot more realistic now.

24. Duplicate the push button layer and position it on the other side of the stopwatch. Go to Edit > Free Transform (CTRL/CMD+T) for a free transform. RIGHT/CTRL-click and choose Flip Horizontal.

> *Holding down the SHIFT key as you drag an object will keep it on the same vertical, horizontal or 45 degree axis.*

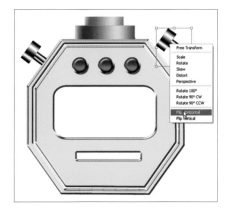

25. Reposition the second button.

3: Making a display

Let's create a new display for the watch. The original one is kind of basic, so we will start from scratch. Relax, it's not too difficult!

26. Choose the main body layer, Layer 1.

27. Using the Magic Wand tool, click inside the display area. This will load a selection in the shape of the display.

28. Create a new layer and name it 'display'.

29. Choose a color for the display background. Here I used 151,186,155; a gray/green color.

30. Fill the selection with the color.

31. Let's add a bit of realism to the display. Go to Filter > Noise > Add Noise and choose the settings shown. Press OK to apply the texture to the display.

32. Use the Type tool to add some numbers to the display. Here I used Impact as the font.

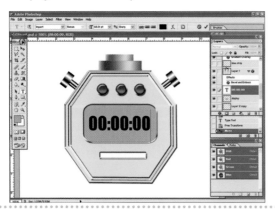

33. Lower the opacity of the layer to 80%. This will make the text blend a little with the background and not appear to be just painted on.

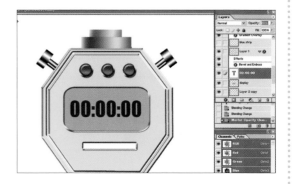

4: Adding a reflection on the screen

To give the display some realism, we'll add a reflection on the glass.

34. CTRL/CMD-click on the display layer to load a selection. Create a new layer above the display and name it 'reflection'. Don't deselect at this point.

35. With white as the foreground color, select the Gradient tool and use a linear gradient, set to Foreground to Transparent. Make sure the Transparency option is checked in the options bar.

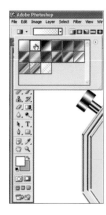

36. Starting halfway up the selection, drag the gradient all the way to the top of the selection.

37. Now we'll resize the gradient; this will help add a rounded look to the display. Go to Edit > Free Transform (CTRL/CMD+T) for a free transform. Grab the bottom center handle and drag the box up.

38. Pull the top down slightly and the sides in slightly too.

39. Press the ENTER key to apply the transformation.

To soften the edges, go to Filter > Blur > Gaussian Blur, using the radius as shown here:

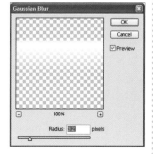

40. Make sure the reflection layer is positioned above the text layer. This will ensure that the text looks like it is beneath the surface of the glass.

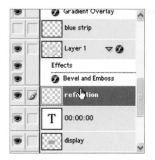

Here's the finished display:

41. Now for the finishing touches. There are still some holes in the body. Let's make them appear like recessed slots in the plastic. Load the selection of the main body.

42. Using the Polygonal Lasso tool with the 'Add to selection' option, make a selection around the perimeter of the inside.

You should now have the octagonal shape loaded as a selection.

43. Create a new layer called 'back' and drag it until it is just above the background and behind all the visible layers.

44. Fill the back layer with a darker tint of the body color.

45. Using the same color, type in some text.

46. Apply an Inner Shadow in the 'Layer Style' dialog to the text to make it appear engraved. Use the following settings:

Here is the end result with a drop shadow applied for some extra effect:

Compare the finished result to the original clip art. There's quite a difference and it wasn't all that hard to do either.

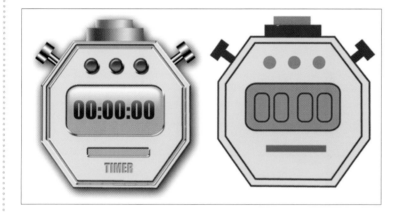

This is a technique that you can adapt and use on all kinds of clip art images. This technique works very well on logos too. It's amazing what a few gradients and layer styles can do to an uninspiring image.

Chapter 10

Exploring the 3D Engine

Photoshop ships with its own built-in 3D rendering engine. Not too many people are aware of this because it's called the **Lighting Effects** filter. This filter, while useful for some simple lighting effects, can be very powerful when combined with an alpha channel.

This technique is one that I have developed for several years and is quite advanced, but with some patience and practice, produces some stunning results.

How it works is as follows. Instead of using a layer to create our image, we'll create it on a channel. The channel will respond just like a layer, except that it's limited to 256 shades of gray. Most of the filters and tools in Photoshop will work in channels.

While painting in the channel, the thing we need to keep in mind is that we are drawing what I call a **3D map**. A 3D map is simply an image that is used as the map for our 3D rendering. You'll need to think in depth as much as you think in shape while drawing the map. The brighter the gray, the higher it will appear on the finished object. Think of 50% gray as being flat. Anything darker is recessed and anything lighter is going to be raised.

White will be the highest point and black will be the lowest point. While we are creating the map, we need to think of height with our grays and not be thinking about shading and color. A smooth gradient will produce the appearance of a smooth slope on the final image.

As you work on this tutorial you'll create an object that has smooth bevels that all fit together seamlessly. It would be impossible to create these bevels with Layer Styles.

1: Creating the shape

1. Create a new document in RGB mode. The size or resolution is not important.

2. Create a new layer and name it. Using the Pen tool, create a path in the shape of your interface, or whatever you want to create. Make sure you choose Paths and not Shape layers from the options bar.

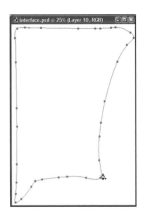

3. Open the Paths palette and save the new path by double-clicking on 'Work Path' in the palette and using the default name (Path 1). We now want to fill the shape. To make a selection, either CTRL/CMD-click on the path thumbnail or click Make Selection in the Paths palette.

4. Fill the new layer with black. Do not deselect at this point.

5. Switch to the channels palette at this point. Click on the 'Save selection as channel' icon in the Channels palette to create a new alpha channel.

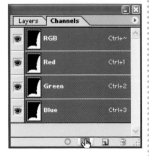

6. You will now see your shape in a new channel called Alpha 1. Click on the new alpha channel in the Channels palette, and then go to Select > Deselect (CTRL/CMD+D) to deselect. You should see a black screen with our shape in white.

7. Because the shade of gray determines the height of an image, what do you think will be the easiest way to produce a rounded beveled edge? Adding a blur to the edges will smooth the black and white line to a softer gray edge. This will be translated as a smooth bevel when we apply the lighting effects. Go to Filter > Blur > Gaussian Blur and set a radius of about 10 pixels.

8. We are now going to apply a blur a second time, but this time use 15 as the radius setting.

This double blur technique will help produce a better looking bevel. It will be softer but with a more clearly defined edge than if we had just applied one large blur.

Now to produce a separate recess into the shape. This is where is gets even more tricky.

9. Select the layer with the main shape on it. Use the **Path Selection** tool to bring up the path. You should see all the anchor points to indicate the path is selected. The anchor points are used together to define the shape of an object.

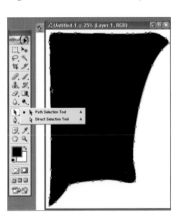

10. Now choose the Pen tool with the minus sign (Delete Anchor Point tool) and click on each of the points to the left and top of the shape to delete the points. We're going to create a path just around the area we want to recess.

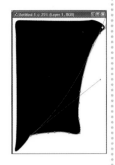

11. Each anchor point has **handles**, and these handles are activated when you click on an actual point. You can adjust the curvy lines by dragging on these handles. Choose the Add Anchor Point tool. If you click on a line between two points with this tool, a new anchor point will be added. But if you click on an existing point, it will activate and the handles will be visible.

12. Use this tool on the handles to create a smooth curve through the shape as shown in these pictures. It may take a bit of practice to get a handle (excuse the pun) on this technique.

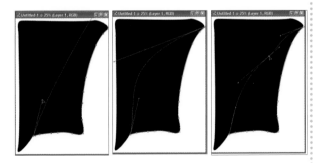

Your final shape should look something like this. If you are using your creative licence and working on something different, that's fine too.

13. Save the path and turn it into a selection in the same way as we did earlier on (CRTL/CMD-click on the path thumbnail or click 'Make selection' in the Paths palette).

14. With the selection active, hide the layer with the shape on it. Create a new layer and fill the selection with a dark/mid gray to a light gray gradient as shown. Name the new layer 'Inside shape'.

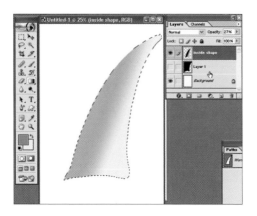

15. We'll want the top part of this shape to blend into the existing interface, and we'll do this by using a layer mask. Click on the 'Add layer mask' icon at the bottom of the Layers palette. Now, vertically fill the top quarter of the mask with a black to white linear gradient to create a smooth blend to white on the top section of the shape.

16. Below is the sort of result you're looking for. Select > Reselect to load the selection. Click Edit > Copy (CTRL/CMD+C) to copy the shape into the clipboard.

17. Don't deselect yet. Open the Channels palette again and click our alpha channel. The selection should still be active over part of our shape as shown.

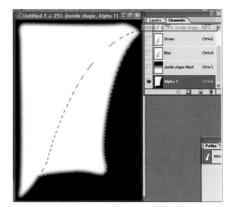

18. Press CTRL/CMD+V or Edit > Paste to paste our gradient into the selection.

19. Let's invert the color so that the top of the selection will be high and the recess slopes downward on the shape. Go to Image > Adjustments > Invert (CTRL/CMD+I) to perform the inversion. Don't deselect yet.

20. As mentioned earlier on, white is the topmost and black is the lowest point on the 3D map. We don't want to make the bottom part go too deep so we will need to lighten up the black a little. Go to Image > Adjustments > Levels (CTRL/CMD+L) and slide the bottom left slider (Below Output levels) to the right until the darkest point on our selection becomes a mid gray.

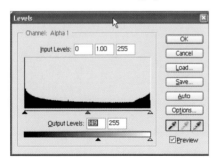

21. Deselect the current selection. You should have something like this now:

22. Let's soften all the edges now. Use a Gaussian Blur with 8.8 as the radius setting (Filter > Blur > Gaussian Blur).

Here is the shape so far. We now want to do a little hand touch-up to get our 3D map just right.

23. Click back to the Layers palette for a moment to load our inside shape selection.

24. When you've made the selection active, return to the Channels palette.

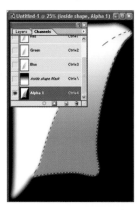

25. Using an Airbrush tool, choose a dark gray soft brush of around 100 pixels and paint a shadow into the left of the selection. Notice how the selection shields the rest of the shape from the painting.

26. Finally, deselect your selection and then choose the Blur tool. Using the default settings, blur all the hard edges and make everything smooth. Pay special attention to the top and make sure there is no hard line showing. When you're finished your channel should look something like this:

2: Rendering the 3D map

Now that our 3D map is created, let's render it as a 3D shape.

1. Create a new layer and fill it with 50% gray. Name the new layer 'shape'.

2. Go to Filter > Render > Lighting Effects, which will open the Lighting Effects filter (mini application). Choose Alpha 1 from the Texture Channel dropdown. You'll see our shape load into the preview pane, with a ring with a center point and four points around it. These are the lighting position controls.

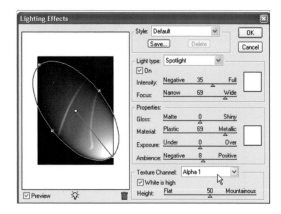

3. Double-click on the color picker under the Cancel button and choose a light orange color. Select Spotlight as the Light type. Click on any of the five points on the lighting position and drag them until you get a nice wide and even color across the entire shape. Ensure that White is high is checked or your image will be inverted.

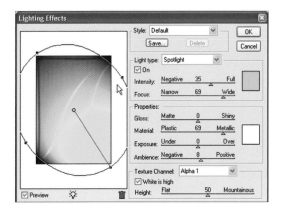

4. Now experiment with the Exposure setting until your lighting is even with no "burned out" areas. To apply the lighting effects, press OK.

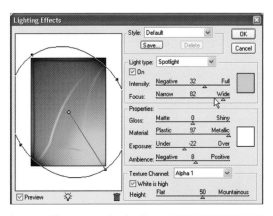

Your image will now render in the gray layer. Notice the smooth curves and slopes; how molded it all appears. All we need to do now is trim the shape – kind of like cutting it out from a mold.

5. Load the selection for the original shape layer by using CTRL/CMD-click in the Layers palette on Layer 1.

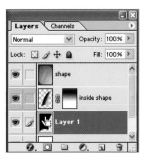

6. Now choose our new shape layer and CTRL/CMD-click to select it. Invert the selection using Select > Inverse.

7. Press DELETE to delete all the unwanted portions of the image.

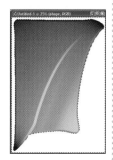

You could now develop the shape and turn it into an interface. This is one of my favorite techniques for creating molded interfaces.

147

I used the same technique for creating the body of this camera image. I know it is a very complex technique, but the results are well worth it.

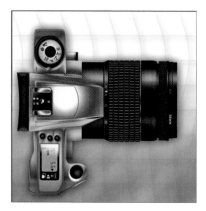

Now for something a lot easier!

3: Using 3D Transform

We're going to use and abuse the 3D Transform tool in this section to produce some quick 3D effects.

Adding text to a rounded surface

Let's add some text to this egg image.

1. Create the text you want to wrap onto the surface.

2. Rotate it into position.

3. We'll have to render the text layer to turn it into a regular layer. Right-click on the layer name in the Layers palette and choose Rasterize Layer from the pop-up menu.

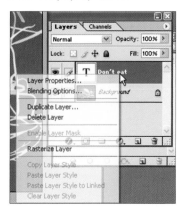

Let's give the text a rounded appearance. Go to Filter > Distort > Spherize, and use 100% and the Normal mode.

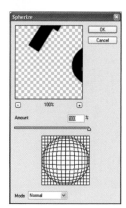

This is the result.

4. Scale the text to fit.

5. Now go to Filter>Render>3D Transform, which will make the 3D Transform filter load. Click on the Sphere tool.

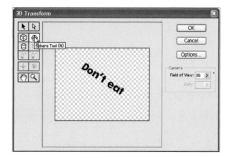

6. Draw a sphere around the text.

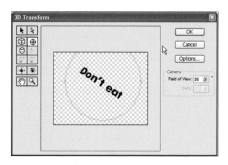

Using the Trackball tool, rotate the sphere downwards. Notice how the text warps in a 3D sphere shape. Click OK.

Trackball tool

149

Here is the result. There is a gray artifact that is created at the top of the egg. This artifact is a bit annoying and needs to be erased. In a little while though, I will show you how to manipulate the artifacts and make them your friends.

7. Draw a selection around the artifact with the Lasso tool and hit DELETE.

8. Reposition the text and change the layer to Overlay mode in the Layers palette for a neat effect.

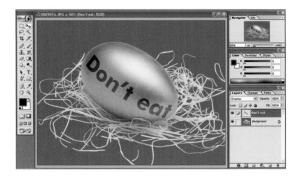

4: Creating 3D shapes

We're now going to quickly create several shapes in 3D using Photoshop. We'll be taking advantage of the artifacts and using them to create shapes that the filter was never intended to do. These are called **primitives** in the 3D world because they are the building blocks for more complex shapes.

Creating a sphere

1. Create a new document sized 800x600 pixels in RGB mode, with black as the background.

2. Create a new layer.

3. Go to Filter > Render > 3D Transform for the new layer. The good thing about the 3D Transform filter is that is needs no content on a layer to work. Choose the Sphere tool and draw a sphere. There's nothing to transform, so what is the point? Hold your horses, and watch this:

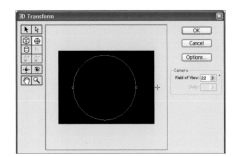

4. Take the Trackball tool and rotate the sphere until the artifact begins to show. Now continue to rotate until the entire shape is an artifact. Click on the Options button.

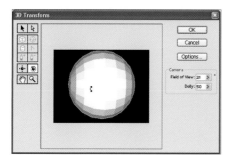

5. Under Resolution choose High. This will make the shape render more detailed and as such will produce a smoother shape. Choose your setting for anti-aliasing. Lower settings will show more of the wireframe while higher settings will produce a smoother curve. Finally, click OK to apply the settings.

6. Now click OK to render our shape onto the layer. Here's our sphere:

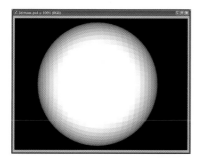

Let's decorate the sphere a bit.

7. Create a new layer and add a shape using the Custom Shape tool. There are three options on the left of the top toolbar: pixels, shape layer and path. Choose pixels. Use black as the color.

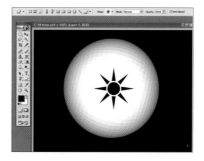

8. Return to the 3D Transform filter again (Filter > Render > 3D Transform). Using the Sphere tool once more, rotate the new shape down and to the left. Click OK to confirm the transformation.

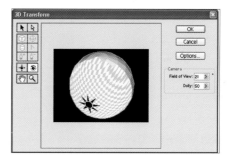

Our image is now rotated like a marking on a golf ball. We're going to keep the layer 2 artifact here to create an interesting effect.

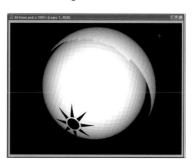

9. Scale the new layer until the artifact fits snugly on top of the sphere.

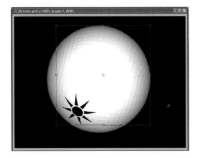

10. Go to Image > Adjustments > Hue/Saturation. Check the Colorize option and slide the Hue slider to add some color. The star shape will be unaffected because it's black.

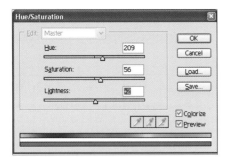

11. Click OK to confirm the changes.

12. Finally, add a default Drop Shadow using the Layer Styles. This is an interesting effect that could be developed for some fun results.

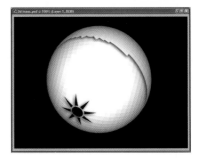

Creating a cube

1. Once again create a new document with black as the background color. Create a new layer and go to Filter > Render > 3D Transform.

2. Choose the Cube tool this time and draw a cube into the preview pane.

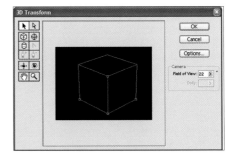

3. Using the Trackball tool, rotate all the way around until all three sides are showing in gray.

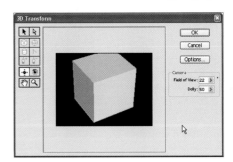

4. You can use the field of view slider to change the size of the cube so that it fits in the window.

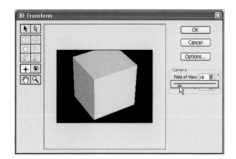

5. Reposition the cube using the Pan Camera controls. Confirm the 3D transformation by clicking OK.

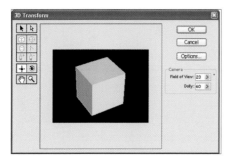

We now have a completed cube. A great thing about the 3D Transform is that it automatically applies some perspective to the shapes making them appear even more realistic.

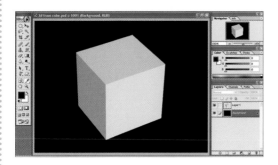

Creating a cylinder

1. Create a new document sized 800x600 pixels in RGB mode, with black as the background. Create a new layer and open the 3D Transform filter (Filter > Render > 3D Transform).

2. Choose the Cylinder tool and draw the shape. Now rotate with the Trackball tool just like we did in the previous two tutorials.

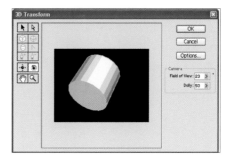

3. Click OK to create a 3D cylinder.

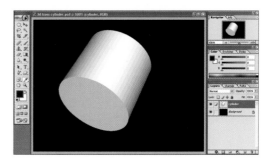

Creating a goblet in 3D

Anyone familiar with 3D will know the term **lathing**. This is when you take a cylinder and carve into it, in the same manner as a lathe would into a piece of wood.

1. Create a new document sized 800x600 pixels in RGB mode, with black as the background. Create a new layer in the new document.

2. Open the 3D Transform filter (Filter > Render > 3D Transform) and choose the Cylinder tool again. Draw a cylinder in the preview pane.

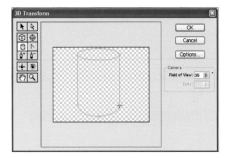

3. Choose the Add Anchor Point tool.

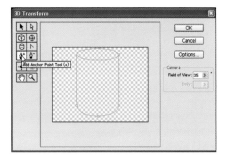

4. Click on the right side of the cylinder (only the right side will work), then click to create an anchor point near the bottom. Create another one between a third and half way up the side.

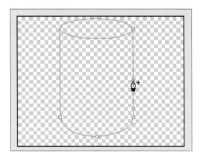

5. Switch to the Direct Selection tool.

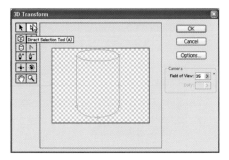

6. Click and drag the first anchor point we created near the bottom. As you drag it in, the left side of the image will mirror your movements.

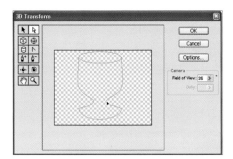

7. Click on the Options button and set the settings to High on both the Resolution and the Anti-aliasing, to produce the smoothest possible render. Click OK to confirm the changes.

8. Using the Trackball tool, rotate the shape all the way around until the entire cup is gray, and then confirm the transformation by clicking OK.

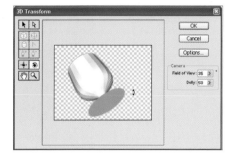

Here's your finished goblet, just waiting for you to dress it up.

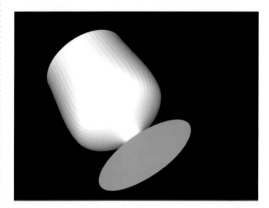

I'm sure your mind is now spinning with lots of exciting ideas. Go ahead and experiment with these new techniques you have learned. Take a break from the book while you try out some ideas of your own and see you next chapter.

Chapter 11

One Hit
Wonders

"Special effects, more special effects!"... It's what everyone is crying out for. So in response to the demand, I've developed this chapter. This is where all kinds of fun and useful effects are revealed. We'll be looking at everything from diamonds, explosions with shockwaves, lighting effects with atmosphere to creating a shadow lens effect.

1: Rap diamonds

Ever since I was moderating the forum for Planet Photoshop, I've had requests for diamond effects. I guess I never found a method I was happy with. Then at PhotoshopCAFE, I had numerous requests for the same effect. People were adding a bit of noise to the text and calling it diamonds. Recently I sat down with Photoshop 7 and decided that I would not leave my computer until I figured out a good method for creating these diamonds. I'm very pleased with the result and you will be too. Get ready to "ice out" your images and text. This is the effect that's used on a lot of rap and hip-hop artists' album cover art.

1. Let's create some text. The key to this effect is to use a good bold font. Here I used a good street font called **Pricedown**. It's available as a free download at www.myfonts.com. So first download the font and install it locally.

2. Create a new document 800x600 in RGB mode. Type in the text nice and big, between 200 and 300 will work well. The color is unimportant at this stage.

3. Render the text so we can apply effects to it by right-clicking on the text in the Layers palette and choosing Rasterize Layer.

4. CTRL/CMD-click on the layer thumbnail to load the selection.

5. Press the D key to reset the foreground and background colors.

6. To set the base tone, choose Filter > Render > Clouds.

7. This is where the diamond effect develops. With the text selection still active, go to Filter > Distort > Glass. Choose 'Tiny Lens' as the texture. Make the scaling relatively small as shown in the screenshot. Move the distortion all the way up and the smoothness all the way down. This process is just a matter of experimenting with the settings to get the best result. Click OK when you've entered the settings.

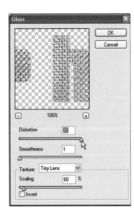

8. We now have the diamond effect on the text. Hit CTRL/CMD+D to deselect.

9. This is almost always used with a golden bevel around it. So, add a Layer Style to the text by pressing the 'Add a layer style' icon at the bottom of the Layers palette. Click on Stroke….

10. Choose a gradient as the fill type and make the stroke about 8 pixels. Actually, you'll want it as wide as you can without the letters overlapping each other. Choose 'Center' as the position.

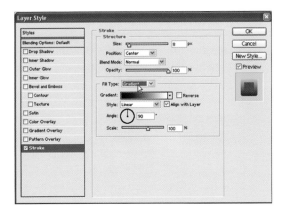

11. Double-click the gradient preview to launch the 'Gradient Editor'.

12. We're going to create a golden gradient. Click on the left and right Color Stops and set them to a gold color. I used hexadecimal number FFCC00.

> To set the color, click the Color Stop and then double-click the box that says 'Color'.

13. Click anywhere below the gradient strip to add a new Color Stop. Choose a color from the 'color' selector.

> To remove a Color Stop, simply drag it off the palette.

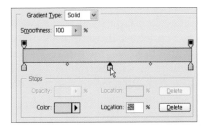

14. Add another two Color Stops. Make one white, one pale yellow and the third should be the same gold color as the end Stops. Your gold gradient should look like the one shown here. Enter a name and click New to save your gradient to the preset library.

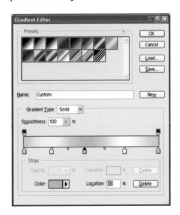

159

15. Change the angle and scale of the gradient until it's similar to what's shown. You'll have to eyeball it and use what looks best for your image. Use the preview on the right to see how it will affect your image.

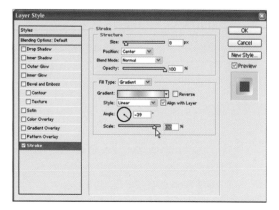

16. Click on the 'Add a layer style' icon at the bottom of the Layers palette and select Bevel and Emboss. To apply the bevel to the stroke we created, choose Stroke Emboss. Copy the settings as shown here. Pay special attention to the gloss contour, this will give it that shiny metallic effect.

17. Click OK to apply the style to our text.

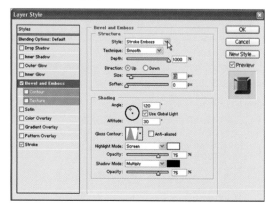

18. Here I've changed the background color to give you a better idea of how it looks. I also added a default Drop Shadow from the 'Layer Style' dialog. We're going to add some sparkles as the finishing touch.

19. Choose the Brush tool and then open the Brushes palette.

20. If the assorted brushes are not already loaded, click the triangle at the top of the Brushes palette for the drop-down menu. Choose Assorted Brushes from the drop-down. When faced with the option to replace or append, choose Append to add the brush collection to your palette and not replace the default brushes.

21. Scroll until you find the large Starburst brush.

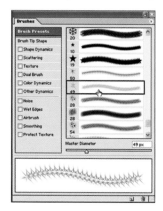

22. Create a new layer. With white as your foreground color and the opacity at 100%, click on the highlight areas to add the starbursts.

> You may need to click twice in the same position to thicken the sparkles.

And here's the final effect. For more examples of this effect in action, visit your local record store and view the hip hop/rap section!

2: An explosion with a shock wave

In the first *Photoshop Most Wanted* book, the explosion tutorial was very popular. Now we're back for more. This time we're going to create a supernova-type explosion with a shockwave shooting out from the center.

1. Create a new document and fill with black, or select black as the background color from the new document menu (it will be the foreground color, if you have the default foreground/background colors selected). Use RGB mode and choose 800x600 pixels (use a higher resolution if you want to create a larger image).

2. Create a new layer and using the Elliptical Marquee tool, draw a circle in the page taking up about half the page.

3. Select the Gradient tool. Create a new gradient in the 'Gradient Editor' and call it 'fire'. Use the same method we did in the last tutorial, except use three Stops of white, yellow and red.

4. Choose a radial gradient with the settings shown here:

5. Fill the circle with the gradient, starting from the center and dragging to the outside along the radius.

6. Use CTRL/CMD+D to deselect. Go to Filter > Blur > Gaussian Blur and enter 11.5 pixels. Click OK.

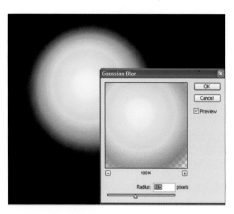

7. Go to Filter > Pixelate > Crystallize and choose 18 as the 'Cell Size'.

8. Go to Filter > Noise > Add Noise and use the settings shown here:

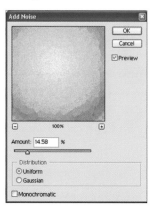

This is what you should have so far:

9. Now let's give it some movement. Go to Filter > Blur > Radial Blur. Use 'Zoom', 100 and 'Best' quality for the smoothest zoom. Click OK.

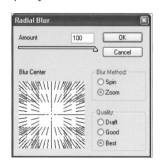

10. Apply the Radial Blur a second time but change the quality to draft. This will create a rougher zoom.

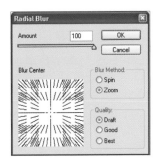

Here's our supernova so far:

11. Duplicate the explosion layer. Change it to Dissolve mode and lower the opacity to 14%.

Now we have the debris coming out from the explosion.

12. It's time for the shock wave. Create a new layer and using the Elliptical Marquee tool, draw an oval shape.

13. Go to Edit > Stroke and choose '5px' and 'Center'. Select white for the color. Click OK and then use CTRL/CMD+D to deselect.

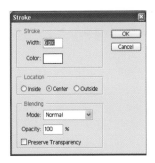

The ring doesn't look too exciting yet. But we're one step away from a 'Wow!'

14. Go to Filter > Blur > Motion Blur. Keep the angle set to 0 and move the distance up to approximately 92. Click OK.

And there we have a shockwave!

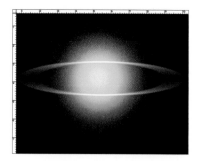

15. Using the Rotate command (CTRL/CMD+T), tilt the shockwave on an angle.

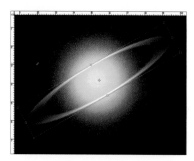

16. We need to hide the part that's behind the explosion. On the shockwave layer create a layer mask.

17. Using a soft black brush, paint away the portion of the ring that would be behind the explosion.

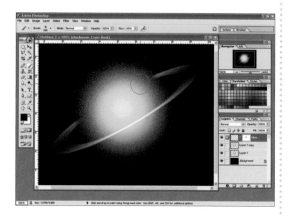

18. Just to finish off the effect, duplicate the shockwave layer. Lower the opacity of the duplicate and scale it up a bit. Then move it down from the original ring just a little bit.

> You can "nudge" the layer (move it 1 pixel at a time) by pressing the arrow keys on the keyboard. Additionally hold down the SHIFT key to nudge in increments of 10 pixels.

There we go: an explosion complete with shockwaves.

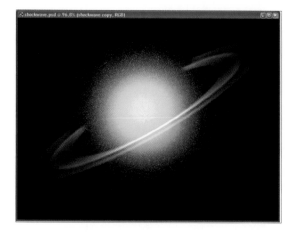

3: Transparent lens shadow

When light is blocked from an object, it creates a shadow on the opposite surface. In most cases the shadow is just a dark blur. What if the object is semi-transparent and there is light shining through it? What would the shadow look like? It's these little details that can really add a strong finishing touch to your images. We're going to create a lens type shadow. Shadow? Well really it's more of a glow.

1. Open the `background.psd` image from the CD.

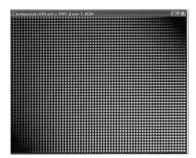

2. In the first Most Wanted book, I showed you how to create a glass sphere. If you don't have it or don't know how to create a glass sphere, then open `sphere.psd` from the CD.

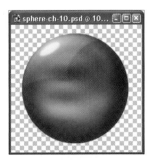

3. Drag the sphere to the background texture.

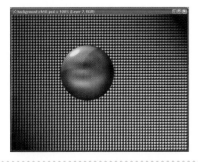

4. Duplicate the sphere layer. Name the copy 'light effect' and move it beneath the sphere layer.

5. Using the Free Transform tool (CTRL/CMD+T), shrink the size by about one third. You may want to hide the original sphere for now, so you can see what you're doing.

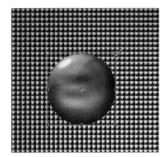

6. Now back to one of my favorite filters: Filter > Blur > Motion Blur. Set the angle at −38 and the distance at 108. Click OK.

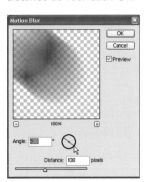

7. Show the sphere layer again.

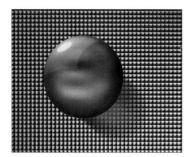

8. Change the Blending Mode of the light effect layer to 'Linear Light'. This Blending Mode is new to Photoshop 7 and acts a bit like an auto dodge/burn. It will dodge everything lighter than 50% gray and burn everything less than 50% gray.

9. See how the light seems to pass through the sphere and shine a colored shadow on the surface. You may want to adjust the shadow layer's position a bit for a better effect.

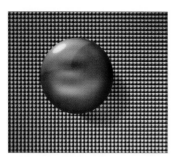

10. Let's enhance the effect. Duplicate the light effect layer. Lower the opacity to 41% and position so that just the "glowing" area is showing.

And here's the finished result; a very realistic effect, if I may say so myself. This technique works best on darker than 50% gray surfaces. For lighter surfaces, experiment with different Blending Modes such as Hard Light.

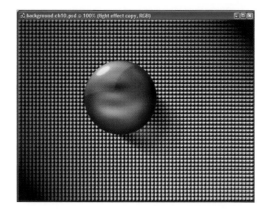

This concludes the one hit wonder parade. We've covered a variety of effects, most of them dealing with light in some fashion or other. It's amazing the amount of impact light has on visual art. Look around at your surroundings and begin to take a mental note of the way that light interacts with your environment. This will help you immensely in creating authentic and authentic artwork. Have fun with these effects, experiment with them and create some interesting variations of your own.

Chapter 12

Web Tricks

Have you ever been surfing the web and hit a page with something so cool you just had to say, "wow!"? I know I have many times. Usually it's just something a bit different or unusually clever that gets your attention. Other times it's just drop-dead stunning graphics.

This chapter is going to focus on a few tricks to help you get the wow factor into your web pages.

1: Multiple rollovers

Ever since I put up the homepage for www.photoshopcafe.com I have had numerous e-mails asking me how I did the rollovers. The page features a row of buttons that have a rollover effect. I also have a screen at the top of the page and when you roll over the buttons, the display in the screen changes to read a description of the link.

This technique is called **multiple rollovers**, **disjointed rollovers** or **remote rollovers**. No matter what you call it, it's a great technique and very easy to create in Photoshop/ImageReady 7.

For this example we're going to use an interface that I created for the tutorials section of the café. You can find the completed interface on the CD (cafetuts.psd). You will find this interface with all the layers intact, for you to experiment with.

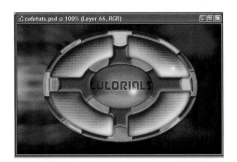

Preparing the rollovers

1. Open cafetuts-noslices.psd from the CD.

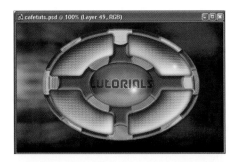

> When you create multiple rollovers, you have to think about what is going to happen and plan it out ahead beforehand. Decide what regions you want to change with the mouse activity and what you want them to change to.

There are two things that are going to change on this interface. When the mouse rolls over a panel, it will change to orange, to make it look like it's charging up (**basic rollover**). At the same time, the text in the center orb will change to the name of the link (**remote rollover**).

The source file on the CD shows all the panels in their rollover state. We'll be editing the blue layers on each panel (**normal state**). When the mouse rolls over each panel, we'll hide the blue layer to reveal the orange layer under each panel.

2. You'll see the colored layers in the set called 'colored rollovers'. Click the eye next to the set to show or hide all the layers.

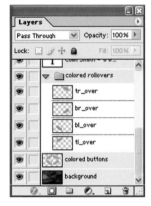

3. Notice that as we hide each colored rollover layer it reveals the orange layer underneath.

The way ImageReady displays rollovers is by simply turning on and off layers and/or styles. So the first thing you need to do to prepare your rollovers is to make the rollover images on separate layers in Photoshop. You should be able to click the eye icon in the Layers palette to see what your rollover will look like in each state.

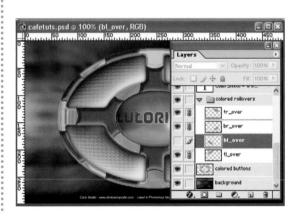

The next thing we will need to do is create the remote rollovers. This relates to what will happen in another portion of the image when the mouse rolls over. In this example, the text in the orb will display differently for each panel.

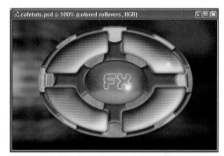

4. You will find the text layers under the text layer set.

This image shows all the text layers turned on at once. Obviously we'll never display the interface like this - we'll display the links one at a time. I just wanted you to see the image with all the rollover images at once to help you better understand the technique we are learning here.

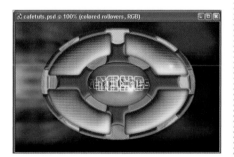

Slicing

Slicing is a term you may have heard and may or may not understand. Let me explain it to you here.

Currently we have one large picture with different layers. When we export it to the web it will become a flattened image. A large flat image is not very flexible. As you know, a rollover effect is created by swapping an image for another image.

We would then have to swap the entire image for a new one for each rollover. That could be done, but would be a huge download. We would have to create five different images, one for the normal default image and one for each of the four rollovers. The smarter way would be to cut the image up (**slice** it) into a series of smaller pictures, and just change the affected portions (slices) of the images. When we add a slice, it tells Photoshop where to cut the image and how many smaller images will be created. When Photoshop creates the new web page (in the final step) it creates all the code that will piece these images together seamlessly like a jigsaw puzzle to give the appearance of one large image.

The rollover effects themselves will also be smaller images that will replace the existing images when the mouse rolls over the defined region (usually a slice). The image inside each slice will be changed to produce the rollover effect.

1. The first thing we need to do is decide how the slices will be created. Try to fit each rollover into one slice. They have to be rectangular in shape and they may overlap each other; however, try to keep this to a minimum as it increases file size.

2. The illustration below shows one of the panel areas and the remote rollover locations highlighted as rectangles. We will want to turn each one into a separate slice. Begin by dragging out guides to help with the slices. Press CTRL/CMD+R to open the rulers. Then just drag the pointer from the rulers to create guides, as shown here.

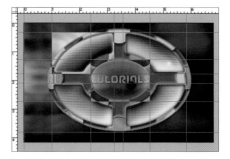

3. Choose the Slice tool, and then click and drag with it to create a slice around the center orb. The slice will break up the page into smaller sections that will load individually. This will enable us to change just a portion of the page at a time and not have to reload the entire page as a rollover image. Notice how Photoshop has added additional slices automatically, surrounding the one we just made. Photoshop will bisect the image to the slice edges, vertically, horizontally or both, to be able to generate the HTML coding.

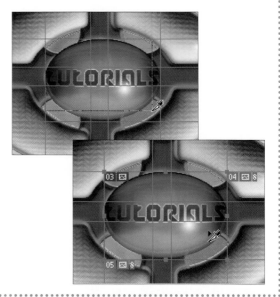

4. Add a slice around each of the rollover areas. The screenshot shows the final sliced image.

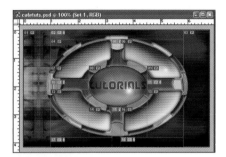

The following image highlights a slice that will be used for one of the rollovers.

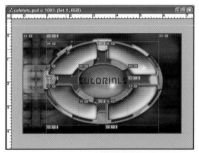

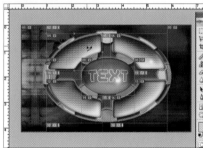

5. We have now done everything necessary to prepare our image. (You could also do the slicing in ImageReady, but sometimes it is useful to do it in Photoshop as, if necessary, you can go back and make changes to your image more easily.) Let's bring it into ImageReady to create the rollovers. Click the 'Jump to ImageReady' button at the bottom of the toolbar (CTRL/CMD+SHIFT+M). This will launch ImageReady and import our image into its window.

The first thing you should do is optimize the slices. Since this tutorial is really about creating rollovers I will make the explanation of optimization very brief.

Optimization is when we tell ImageReady the quality of the images to produce. We'll need to produce lower quality images for the web in order to cut load time. A balance of quality versus speed is required when optimizing. Often you can reduce the quality of a slice without it really being visually noticeable. Use higher quality for CD-ROM projects because they have a faster download speed. A basic rule of thumb is to use GIFs for text and images with flat color and JPEGs for photos and complex shading. I have just finished writing another book for friends of ED called *From Photoshop to Dreamweaver: 3 Steps to Great Visual Web Design* which covers slicing and optimization in a lot more detail.

6. Select a slice with the Slice Select tool. Also click on the Optimized preview tab.

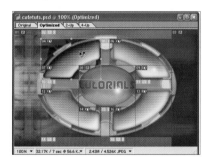

7. In the Optimize palette, choose JPEG and lower the Quality slider until you just begin to see a little image degradation. Try to keep it under 50%. Repeat this optimization process for each slice, including the slices that don't have rollovers attached.

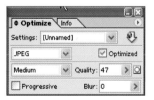

Creating the rollovers

Now that we have all the slices created and the optimization done, it's time to create the rollovers.

1. Open the Rollovers palette. Choose the slice that is over the top left panel of the interface. Click the 'Create rollover state' icon at the bottom of the Rollovers palette.

You'll now see the **Over State**. This is the image that will be created for our rollover effect.

2. Open the Layers palette and hide the blue layer to reveal the orange underneath. This is what the rollover will look like. For the sake of understanding, I will call this the master rollover.

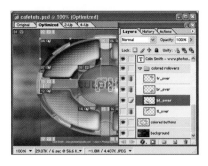

The thumbnail display in the Rollovers palette will be updated to show the rollover image. (This screen shot shows all four rollovers for the entire interface.)

Now we'll create our remote (secondary) rollover.

3. Turn off the tutorials layer to hide the text that says 'tutorials' and click the eye next to fx in the text layer set. This will now display 'fx' in the center orb.

When a rollover state is selected in the Rollovers palette, ImageReady will change all the slices that have modifications (secondary) and not just the 'master' slice. The master slice will act as the trigger for the mouse. If the mouse rolls over a secondary slice, nothing will happen.

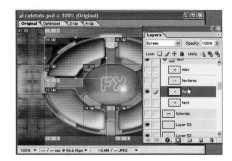

4. If you wish to go to a new page when the mouse clicks on the interface, select the Slice palette and assign a link in the URL field.

5. Repeat these steps for the remaining three buttons and remember to reveal the correct layers to change the text in the center for each one. When you are done, click the Preview button in the toolbar.

6. You can now roll your mouse over each button to test the rollovers. You'll have to pause on each button for a few seconds while ImageReady loads the rollovers. If any of the buttons don't rollover correctly, go back to the Rollovers palette and make sure that the correct layers are shown/hidden for each state.

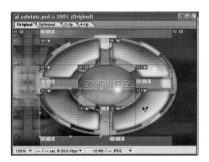

7. Click the 'Preview in Default Browser' icon to see what the interface will look like in a web browser.

8. The browser will launch with a functioning interface, and some interesting statistics, including the coding for the rollovers, on the page.

9. Once you have tested that the interface works in a web browser, you can export it as a web page. ImageReady will create all the code and an HTML page for you. Go to File > Save Optimized As, choose a folder to export to and click Save. You'll now see the HTML document and a folder containing all the sliced images.

10. Launch the HTML document in your web browser.

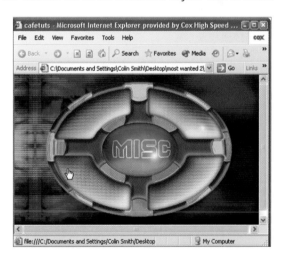

Use this technique on your own creations and create some great interactive web pages and interfaces for your websites and multi-media projects.

2: Creating an animated slideshow

We're now going to create an animated slideshow. This is not just a basic slideshow – we're going to use ImageReady's tweening feature to create TV-like fades between the images. We'll then export the whole slideshow as one animated GIF.

This technique will work best for kiosks, CDs and broadband. It will also work for a regular web page, but I would advise using a smaller image for this purpose to help keep the file size down.

1. Open the interface called `animation.psd` from the CD in ImageReady. You'll see that it is all in three layers: the frame, a black filler, and the background.

We are going to turn the background into a matte. This will mean that all the pictures we add will not have to be cropped – they will merely need to be dropped into the layer beneath the interface.

2. CTRL/CMD-click on the interface layer to load the selection.

3. Select the Background layer in the Layers palette.

4. Go to Select > Inverse or CTRL/CMD+SHIFT+I, so that everything will be selected except for the area around the interface shape.

5. Go to Layer > New > Layer via Copy or press CTRL/CMD+J. This copies the information from the background and places it on a new layer in the shape of the selection. Name the new layer 'matte'.

6. Drag the matte layer to the top of the Layers palette.

7. Make a selection around the window area with the Rectangular Marquee tool.

8. Press the DELETE key to remove the selection. You can now see all the way through to the black layer. This area will become our screen.

9. Drag your images into the document. Here we have only used two to demonstrate the technique. You can choose as many as you wish, but remember, the more images, the longer it will take to load in the browser. If you plan on putting this on a web page or using several images, I recommend resizing and optimizing the images now. Choose any images you want. I have used two pictures of my vacation in Venice. They are Venice-1.jpg and Venice-2.jpg, and can be found on the CD.

10. Drag the images under the interface layer. The new matte we created will hide all the edges of the pictures.

11. Resize and position the top image.

12. Hide the top image and reposition and size the next one. If you are using more than two images, continue with each image until they are all in position and ready for the animation.

13. Show the top image again. Click on the Animation palette and then click the 'Duplicate current frame' icon to add a new frame, frame 2.

At the moment both frames are identical.

14. Hide the top image again to reveal the second image.

We now have a two-frame animation. If we wanted a simple slideshow, we could just set the delay for each frame at 2-5 seconds and we would be done. However, we want to create a smooth fade between the pictures.

15. Click the arrow at the top right of the Animation palette and choose Tween from the drop-down menu.

16. ImageReady is now going to create a fade between the two frames. Tweened frames are all the in-between frames that smooth out an effect, in this case, fading one image into another. Tweens were really added for motion tweens, but they work well in this example too. Use the settings shown in the screenshot:

17. Click OK and all the new frames will be added.

Since this is a looping animation, we need a smooth transition back to the original image. We will add the tweened frames to the end of the animation and reverse them to transition in reverse to the original image.

18. Select all the tween frames: Frames 2 through 6. To select more than one frame at a time, click on the first frame you want to select, hold down the SHIFT key, click on the last frame and all the ones in between will also be selected.

> *Holding down the CTRL/CMD key and clicking allows for selecting frames that are not adjacent.*

19. Choose 'Copy Frames' from the drop-down menu in the Animation palette.

20. Select the last frame.

21. Now choose paste frames. The 'Paste Frames' dialog will appear, asking you how you want to paste the frames. Choose Paste After Selection.

22. The frames will now be added. Do not deselect them yet, as we still need to reverse this portion of the animation.

23. From the drop-down menu, choose Reverse Frames. All the selected frames will now be reversed in order.

24. Press the play button on the Animation palette to watch the animation play. It will probably be a bit slower and more jumpy in ImageReady than in your web browser.

25. When you have finished previewing press the stop button. You'll have noticed that the fades are looking good, but the animation needs to pause for a few seconds on each of the images.

26. Select frame 7, which is the second image.

27. Click on the '0 sec' and a drop-down will appear. This is where you choose the delay. We will use a 2 second delay. This will cause the animation to pause for 2 seconds on this frame.

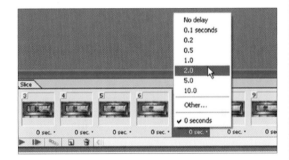

28. We also need to pause the first picture on frame 1. However, we want the animation to begin playing right away. So what we will do is copy the frame, paste it to the end of the animation and add the delay there.

29. Once pasted we'll have a new frame, frame #13.

30. Add the 2-second delay to the new frame.

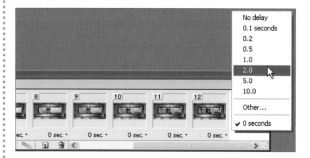

31. In the Optimize window change the file type to GIF and reduce the colors to 128 to reduce the file size.

> Note that you'll only be able to choose the GIF option, as JPEGs don't support animation.

32. Click the 'Preview in Default Browser' icon.

32. You'll now see the animation launch in your web browser. Notice how much smoother it appears now.

33. Finally, go to File > Save Optimized As to export your animated GIF. If you plan on using this in a web page, I recommend cropping the image as tightly as possible and reducing the overall size. This will make the file size shrink significantly.

There is still some wasted space around the interface itself. In this next tutorial you will find out how to animate in the smallest possible space and make it appear as part of a larger image. This is a great way to add some interest to a web page.

3: Animating portions of an image

It's possible to take what we have learned in this chapter and take a large image and animate portions of it. This gives the impression that the entire image is animated, but really only carefully selected portions are.

This will involve a bit of trickery, as our image will push ImageReady beyond its programming and we'll have to fool it a bit. Don't worry though, I'll take you step-by-step through the whole process.

I have stripped down one of my 100% Photoshop creations for this tutorial. The Image is called `Alien animation.psd`. Open this file now.

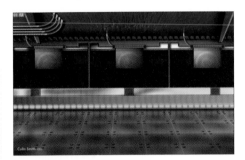

I have the Station itself as the matte. Layer 0 is the background. We'll animate a shooting star through the windows (Star layer). We also have a layer set called TV. This set contains the TV screens. We are going to animate some static on two of the screens.

You'll see four layers called noise. Creating the static is easy. I simply made a selection the size of the TV screens, made new layers and ran a Noise filter on them (Filter > Noise > Add Noise). I made two noise layers for each screen. By making a two-frame animation between the two noise layers, it will give the illusion of TV static.

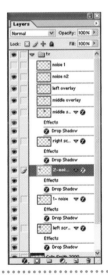

This is what the finished animation will look like with the TV static and the shooting star moving in through the windows.

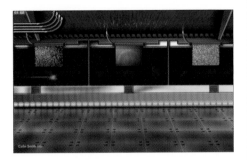

Defining the slices

1. The first thing we need to do is define the areas that will be animated. We will do this with slices. Make a slice around each of the TV screens.

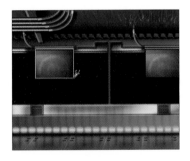

2. Using the Slice tool, make a slice along the bottom part of the window. We have now defined the three animation zones. The rest of the image will be static except for these three areas. The challenge we have is that ImageReady only has one Animation palette and no timeline. This means that it can only create one animation per image by default. We're going to be cunning here and make ImageReady think we're creating rollovers, thus we can use the rollover states to create new animations. Then we're going to swap out the rollover images and make the animation the default image. This may sound confusing, but all will become clear as we work through the example.

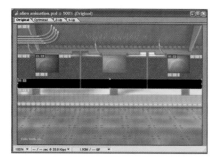

3. Open the Rollovers palette and choose the palette options. Check Include animation frames. Our animations will now show on the Rollovers palette. Don't worry, we're creating animations and not rollovers, you didn't miss anything. We are going to use the rollover tools to fool ImageReady.

4. Use the Slice Select tool and select the window animation zone.

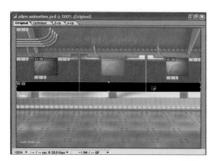

5. Add a new state to the window slice. Don't select the state, stay on the default state.

6. Make the star layer visible.

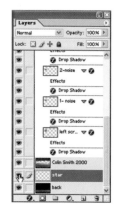

7. Let's define the start point for the animation. Drag the star off to the left until it is totally out of the canvas area. Hold the SHIFT key as you drag to keep it on a horizontal plane.

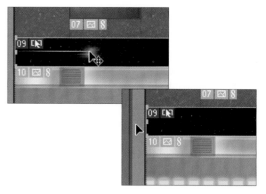

8. Let's now define the ending of the animation. Create the second frame.

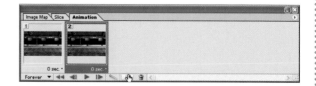

9. Drag the star all the way across to the right-hand side of the image, until it is just off the canvas. Remember to hold the SHIFT key. This will ensure that our animation follows a smooth horizontal path.

10. Just like we did before, we'll add some tweened frames. Select the options from the Animation palette and open the 'Tween' dialog. Use the following settings:

11. Test the animation and the shooting star should now travel across the screen .

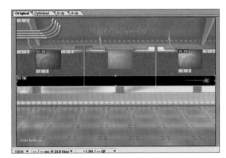

12. The animation is looping and the shooting star is constantly moving. Set a delay time of 10 seconds to the last frame. This will cause it to pause at the end of the animation before looping.

13. Let's animate the TV screens now. Select one of the screens with the Slice Select tool. You'll notice that the Animation palette still contains the star animation. This is the problem we were talking about earlier. Here comes the workaround. Don't you just love pushing a program beyond its natural capabilities?!

14. Add a new rollover state to the TV slice in the Rollovers palette (Alien animation_05). Select the Over State. You'll see the Animation palette is empty now, all ready for us to use to prepare our second animation.

15. Notice that the TV slice now has a small icon next to the slice number to indicate that there is a rollover attached.

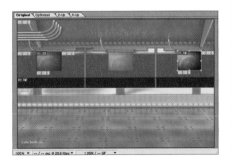

16. Select the noise 1 layer in the Layers palette and make sure it is visible. Then create a new frame in the Animation palette.

17. Now hide the noise 1 layer and show the noise 2 layer. That's it! The static animation is set up.

18. Repeat the same steps for the second TV slice.

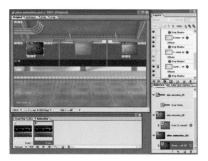

19. In the Optimize palette, define each slice as a JPEG, except for our three animation zones, which you should set to GIF. This will ensure that only the three slices will be animated as it's impossible to attach an animation to a JPEG. Take note of the slice names of our three zones now, they're 3, 5 and 9. If yours are different write them down now. We'll use this information in a minute.

20. Click the 'Preview in Default Browser' icon. You'll see an alert message saying ImageReady will save only currently selected frames for the JPEG images. That is exactly what we wanted – otherwise the entire page would be animated. This trick will force ImageReady to animate only our three zones. Click OK.

> Be sure that the three slices we want to animate are not in the list (mine were 3, 5, and 9). If you see them there, then you have made a mistake somewhere and need to backtrack and fix it.

21. You can now preview the animation in your web browser.

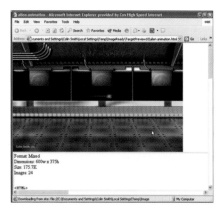

You'll notice that the screens will only animate when the mouse rolls over them. This is not a surprise because we created the animations on the rollover state.

Remember how rollovers work? One image swaps to another image on mouse activity. This means that there is an animated GIF somewhere that shows on rollover. Actually there is an animated GIF for each of the three zones. The shooting star is fine because it's running by default. What we need to do is swap the static images on the TV screens for the animated GIFs.

We're going to do this in two ways. The first method will be for those of you who know some HTML. The second method will be for those of you who are afraid of code. Choose the method that best suits you.

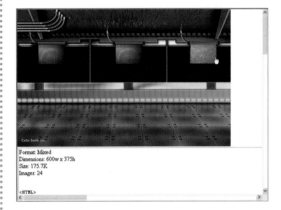

22. No matter what method you use, you will need to save the image and its HTML page. Go to File > Save Optimized As. Choose a directory and you will see an HTML document and a folder with images. Let's make our modification so that all the animations will run simultaneously.

Method 1 - Changing the code
If you use Dreamweaver, GoLive, Frontpage or some other HTML editor, just swap out the images in the tables using those programs. If you want to do some quick HTML hand-coding, follow along.

1. Open the HTML document in Notepad, or SimpleText.

2. Look for the table. It will be between the `<TABLE>` tags.

3. Now look for the table cell `<TD>` that contains our first slice `alien-animation_03`.

4. We're looking for `<IMG NAME="alien-animation_03" SRC="images/alien-animation_03,gif"Width=76 HEIGHT=57 BORDER=0>`. This is the only code needed to display our image. All the other code between the `<TD>` tags refers to the rollover. We'll need to locate the name of the rollover image. It's `alien-animation-over.gif` (our animated gif). ImageReady adds the '-over' to all the rollover images.

5. All we need to do is replace the `IMG SRC=(target)` with the animated GIF and then delete all the redundant code for this table cell, leaving only our animated GIF behind.

```
ONMOUSEOUT="changeImages('alien_animation_01',
'images/alien-animation_01.jpg', 'alien_animation_02',
'images/alien-animation_02.jpg', 'alien_animation_03',
'images/alien-animation_03.gif', 'alien_animation_04',
'images/alien-animation_04.jpg', 'alien_animation_05',
'images/alien-animation_05.gif', 'alien_animation_06',
'images/alien-animation_06.jpg', 'alien_animation_07',
'images/alien-animation_07.jpg', 'alien_animation_08',
'images/alien-animation_08.jpg', 'alien_animation_09',
'images/alien-animation_09.gif', 'alien_animation_10',
'images/alien-animation_10.jpg', 'alien_animation_11',
'images/alien-animation_11.jpg'); return true;">
                                        <IMG
NAME="alien_animation_03"
SRC="images/alien-animation_03.gif" WIDTH=76 HEIGHT=57
BORDER=0></A></TD>
                    <TD ROWSPAN=2>
```

6. Replace the `IMG NAME` and `SRC` with the `-over` name. Since the only thing that is different is the `-over` on the name, type it into the code. The highlighted code is all we will need between the `<TD>` tags.

```
ONMOUSEOUT="changeImages('alien_animation_01',
'images/alien-animation_01.jpg', 'alien_animation_02',
'images/alien-animation_02.jpg', 'alien_animation_03',
'images/alien-animation_03.gif', 'alien_animation_04',
'images/alien-animation_04.jpg', 'alien_animation_05',
'images/alien-animation_05.gif', 'alien_animation_06',
'images/alien-animation_06.jpg', 'alien_animation_07',
'images/alien-animation_07.jpg', 'alien_animation_08',
'images/alien-animation_08.jpg', 'alien_animation_09',
'images/alien-animation_09.gif', 'alien_animation_10',
'images/alien-animation_10.jpg', 'alien_animation_11',
'images/alien-animation_11.jpg'); return true;">
                                        <IMG
NAME="alien_animation_03-over"
SRC="images/alien-animation_03-over.gif" WIDTH=76
HEIGHT=57 BORDER=0></A></TD>
                    <TD ROWSPAN=2>
```

183

7. Highlight all the code after the `<TD>` tag to just before the `<IMG NAME>` tag as shown.

8. Press DELETE and your code should look something like this. Take out the `</A>` tag before the closing `</TD>` tag.

```
ALT=""></TD>
            <TD>
<IMG NAME="alien_animation_03-over"
SRC="images/alien-animation_03-over.gif" WIDTH=76
HEIGHT=57 BORDER=0></TD>
            <TD ROWSPAN=2>
            <IMG NAME="alien_animation_04"
```

Save the page as `alien-animation2.html`. It's always a good idea to save a copy of a page after you have altered the code. This way you can revert to the original version if the modified page doesn't work correctly. Test the page in the browser. One of the TVs should now be animated as well as the shooting star. If you have an error, go back and check the code again carefully.

9. Now do the same thing for the second TV screen on the same page we just saved. This code method is the cleanest way to modify the animations.

Method 2 - Switch image names

This second method requires no coding. We're going to replace the static image with the animated GIF by renaming.

1. Open the `Images` folder. You'll find `alien-animation_05.gif` and `alien-animation_05-over.gif`. Select `alien-animation_05.gif`.

2. Rename it to `alien-animation_05-old.gif`.

3. Select `alien-animation_05-over.gif`.

4. Rename to `alien-animation_05.gif`. The animation will now work on the page. The only problem is that if the mouse rolls over the screen the rollover will show no image.

5. To correct that, rename `alien-animation_05-old.gif` to `alien-animation_05-over.gif`. We have effectively switched out the two images. When the mouse rolls over the screen the static will stop and the screen will clear. This is a great way to create buttons for your web page – the name of your link could be on the screen.

> If you want to maintain the static all the time, make two copies of the animated GIF and name them `alien-animation_05-over.gif` and `alien-animation_05.gif`.

6. Repeat the renaming for the second TV screen.

7. Launch your page in the web browser and watch all three animations run together.

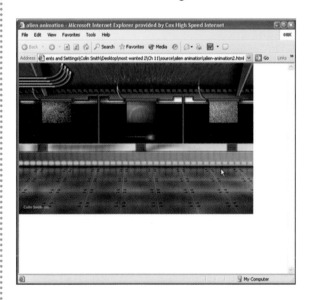

I hope this chapter has given you some good techniques to add some interactivity to your web pages. Most of all, I hope it has acted as a primer and got you thinking about all kinds of effects you can experiment with on your own.

Chapter 13

Photo
Manipulation

"The camera never lies." Very true, but with Photoshop we can 'bend the truth' a little. In fact, it's possible to modify and doctor any image. We can break the laws of physics and defy gravity. For example, here's an image of a car that I modified to make it look like it's hovering:

In this chapter we're going to work with photos and produce some interesting results. These techniques will come in useful for preparing advertising, web page design and just plain old fun.

1: Extracting an image from the background

Before you can make the most of these modifications, you'll need to learn how to extract an image from its background. Photoshop ships with a useful tool called the **Extract tool**. I'm now going to show you a quick no-nonsense way to use it.

1. Begin with the image you want to pull from the background. Here I've used a surfer (28019.jpg). You can use any image – the technique is exactly the same.

2. Make a copy of the layer and hide the original Background layer. This technique will discard the background and it always pays to keep a copy just in case. I can't emphasize it enough, always keep an original of everything!

3. Launch the Extract filter by selecting Filter > Extract.

Here's how the Extract filter works: you highlight the outline of the image that you want to extract, and then it does its magic. Using the average colors on the outline, Extract will try to decide what is foreground and what is background and discard the background. This tool works very well and can even isolate individual hairs. Now to walk through it.

4. Select the Edge Highlighter tool.

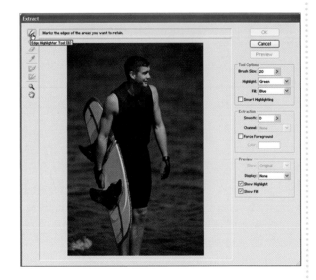

5. This image has sharp edges, so make the brush size smaller. You would use a larger brush size for softer areas such as fur and hair. I'll explain more in the next step.

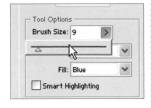

6. Begin to highlight the edges, but before going too far, read the tips below.

Extract will look at the highlighted edge as the 'deciding zone'. This is where it will decide to keep or discard – so obviously, the thinner the line the sharper the extract. Make sure the entire edge is covered. A larger brush size will make a larger 'deciding zone' and is useful for softer more complex extraction. Now that you know that, the edge I've used here is too large:

There's a feature called Smart Highlighting. You can check it on in the menu if you wish but I prefer this method: when you hold down the CTRL/CMD key while drawing, Extract will temporarily turn on the Smart Highlighting mode. Extract will attempt to find the edges and produce a thinner line right on it.

7. Using the tips above, highlight the entire outline of the image.

8. There's no way that Extract would know which part of the image you want to keep and which part you want to discard. It's smart, but it still can't read your mind. So, select the Paint Bucket tool and mark the area you want to keep by clicking inside the area. It will fill with blue (by default – you can change it).

9. Click OK. You'll now be returned to your Photoshop document, without its background.

10. It's looking pretty good, but not perfect. Use the Eraser tool to delete any stragglers you may see.

11. In some cases there are parts extracted that you may want to keep, like the missing parts on our subject's left forearm – he may want them! Select the History Brush from the toolbox.

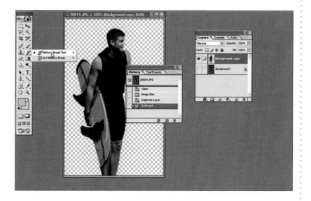

12. Open the History palette and choose a history state to paint with. This is like painting an undo to any point in the palette. Choose the state just before the Extract. Check the box next to the desired state and you should see an icon of a brush and an arrow.

13. Using small brush sizes, paint the lost parts back in. You may want to zoom into the image for more detail.

After a little work, here's the final image:

You can now drag and drop it onto any background you choose.

2: Adding a person to a background

Now that we know how to extract a person, let's look at some techniques to make a convincing photo manipulation.

There's another option for extracting your images. Hemera Technologies have a product called **PhotoObjects**. These surprisingly affordable collections contain thousands of images that have already been extracted. Look on the CD for 100 free sample images.

1. For this example we'll be using one of the PhotoObject images on the disk called: woman model 3.psd. Open it up now.

We'll also be using a website that I made for a fictitious band called Hazardous Waste. They want to advertise the new site in a magazine, so we're going to create the ad.

> The images here are 72ppi for learning purposes. In the real world, you would use 300ppi for a print ad.

2. Open waste_site.psd from the CD.

3. Using Free Transform (CTRL/CMD+T), right-click and choose Distort.

4. Drag the corners and distort the page to make it appear as if it's tilted in space as shown.

5. Fill the background with white. Drag the image of the model into the document.

> If you hold the SHIFT key while dragging into a new document, your item will be automatically centered.

6. Resize and position the model so that it looks like she's sitting on the page.

7. Now we need to add something to tie the two images together and make it believable. A cast shadow will be perfect. Duplicate the model layer, but leave the duplicate layer alone and return to Layer 2 to apply the shadow. Make a selection of the model and fill the selection with black.

8. Still on Layer 2, once again use Free Transform. Choose Distort again.

9. Drag the top part of the shadow to make it appear as though it's cast across the page at the same angle as the web page. Press the ENTER key to apply.

10. A real shadow is soft and fades the further it gets from the subject. Go to Filter > Blur > Gaussian Blur…. I like to use a setting of 5 to soften the edges of a cast shadow.

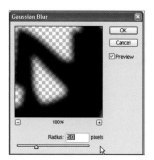

Now the edges are looking better. Lower the opacity to 63%

11. Let's fade the shadow so that it loses intensity the further it gets from the model. Click the 'Add layer mask' icon to add a mask to the shadow layer.

12. Choose the Gradient tool, and select the default colors (press the D key). Use the foreground to background linear gradient.

13. Drag the gradient from the middle of the shadow and upwards until you are about an inch off the top. You should get a result like the one shown. If not, just keep reapplying the gradient until you're satisfied with the result.

14. You may need to reduce the opacity on the shadow layer to suit your tastes and your background.

15. Finally add some type and you're done. A nice clean typeface will look good; in this case I've used Impact. When you have an eye-catching image, sometimes it's good to use a simple typeface. This helps to avoid an overly busy image, which confuses the eye and gives it nowhere to rest.

A good magazine ad should be clean, with impact to catch the attention, but without overwhelming the senses. Look at the ads that are really busy with lots of images and type on them, do you really think they can get their message across in one glance? No. A good ad will already have delivered its message before the reader has even decided whether to read it or not.

3: Combining two images together and making it look convincing

Look at these steps. Imagine how much it would cost to hire a stuntman to jump off them on a motorcycle. Then take the costs of a photographer with a quick eye to capture the moment. We'll save some money and perhaps a few bruises with this tutorial.

1. Open the steps image on the CD that you want to add the motorcycle to, `1403.jpg`. We'll call this the base image.

2. Now open the Hemera image `couple on Motorcycle 3.psd` from the CD.

3. Drag the motorcycle image into the base image.

4. Resize, position and rotate to make it look like we're jumping off the steps.

A big part of combining images is making the tones match. I recently saw a big Hollywood movie with some scenes that looked so fake because the shadow tones didn't match on the foreground and background images. I was thinking, just adjust the tone curve and this would look 300% more real.

5. With the motorcycle layer selected, open the 'Curves' dialog box (Image > Adjustments > Curves…).

6. Adjust the curve to make the images fit better together. Left is shadows and right is highlights. Pull up to brighten and down to darken anywhere on the tone curve.

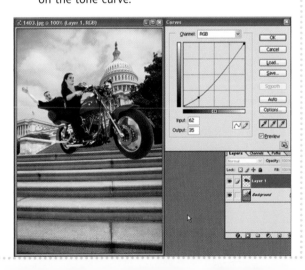

> *Another dead giveaway is when the saturation doesn't match on the two images. Saturation is the intensity of the color. An under-saturated image looks like it has faded in the sun, whereas an over-saturated image looks too fake and plastic. Notice that the motorcycle appears more saturated than the base image.*

7. Go to Image > Adjustments > Hue/Saturation… to open the dialog box. Move the 'Saturation' slider to the left to lower the color saturation of the selected layer until it matches the background image.

Other things to watch for include:

- Film grain – If the grains don't match it will look doctored. The fix for that is to add some noise to the lowest grain image.

- Lighting – Make sure that the lighting is coming from the same angle. Carefully added shadows can fix that, as you're about to see.

- Wind direction – This is easy to overlook. Imagine trees blowing one way and an umbrella bursting open the in opposite direction.

- There may be other little things too. Examine your image carefully and look for things that are out of place, such as reflections, perspective, ambient lighting and so on.

8. Let's add a little bit of a blur to the motorcycle to imply movement. Duplicate the motorcycle layer.

9. On the duplicated layer add a motion blur by selecting Filter > Blur > Motion Blur…. Adjust the angle to match the movement direction. Make sure to move the blurred layer underneath the original motorcycle layer.

10. Drag the blurred layer to the left so that it trails the image.

> *I lowered the opacity to 38% to make the blur a little more subtle. One of the keys to realism is subtlety.*

11. We'll now add the drop shadow to make it look like the motorcycle is occupying space in the same image as the steps. Duplicate the motorcycle layer and select the copy. Rename it 'shadow', and rename the other layers more intuitively while you're at it! Drag the shadow layer below the cycle layer.

12. With a selection of the motorcycle generated, fill the shadow layer with black.

13. Deselect and then add the 5-pixel blur by going to Filter > Blur > Gaussian Blur... and entering 5 in the **'Radius'** box.

14. Drag the shadow underneath the image, until it's cast on the steps.

We now have a drop shadow, but it needs some work to make it look realistic. If you've ever watched the way a shadow 'creeps' on steps you'll know what I mean.

15. Hide the motorcycle layer for now. Choose the shadow layer.

16. Drag a selection across the part of the shadow that extends above the steps. We're going to remove the shadow from this region. (Note: If the image was front lit, then keeping the shadow on the background portion would be okay, but looking at the existing shadows on the image we can determine that the sun's position is above and to the right.)

17. Press DELETE to remove the pixels in the selection.

18. Make a selection of the shadow from the top step face, downwards.

19. Move the shadow to the right just a little.

20. We could move everything one segment at a time, but here's a quicker way. Make a selection on the top of the next step down using the Polygonal Lasso tool.

21. Holding down the SHIFT key (to add to selection), select the tops of the rest of the steps.

22. Press CTRL/CMD+T to open the 'Free Transform' dialog box.

23. Right-click and press Skew. We're going to distort the shadow on the tops of the steps to make it look like the shadow is actually wrapping on the steps and not just pasted on.

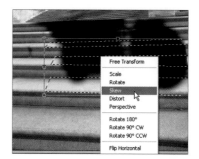

24. Drag the mouse to the left so that the shadow is falling in the opposite direction to the sun angle.

25. Click OK to apply. Don't deselect yet. Press CTRL/CMD+SHIFT+J to move the selected pixels to their own layer (Layer > New > Layer via Cut). Rename the new layer 'shadow 2'. Deselect now.

26. We now have a rough shadow. All that's left is to soften the shadow and blend it in to make it look realistic.

27. Select the shadow 2 layer.

28. Add a 3.2-pixel Gaussian Blur.

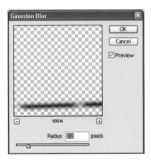

29. Also apply the same blur to the shadow layer.

> To reapply the previous filter with the same settings, press CTRL/CMD+F – be sure to select the other shadow layer first.

30. Lower the opacity of the shadow layer to 50%.

31. Lower the opacity of the shadow 2 layer to 77%. The reason we made this higher is because shadows will appear to fall darker directly on top of objects.

32. Turn the motorcycle layer back on and admire your handiwork. Doesn't the shadow add a lot to the image? Carefully applied shadows and highlights can be used to great effect to pull images together.

I'm sure you've had fun in this chapter. Photo manipulation is one of the most fun things in Photoshop. You've also learnt some good principles of image matching and photo manipulation. Use these techniques for all kinds of images.

You've learned how to weld parts of images together and create very realistic-looking shadows. You've also learned a number of things to watch out for when combining images and some techniques to counter them and produce believable-looking photo manipulations.

Photo manipulation is a very important Photoshop skill to possess. I actually picked up a lot of my illustration techniques this way.

Chapter 14

Transparency Effects

Isn't it fascinating how objects appear to distort through lenses, glass and gel? This chapter is going to show you how to produce some popular and requested transparency effects. We're not only going to create the lenses, we're going to distort the background behind them.

1: Magnifying glass

In this tutorial we are going to create a magnifying glass and then cause it to interact with the background behind it.

1. Start with this background image that I prepared earlier, or use your own. You'll find my file on the CD as `Background.psd`.

2. Create a new layer called 'ring'. This is where we're going to build our magnifying glass.

3. Using the Elliptical Marquee tool, create a circle and fill it with white. Make it as large as you want the lens to be. I've made it just under half of the image height.

Hold down the SHIFT *key to constrain to a perfect circle.*

4. Let's turn the circle into a ring. Go to Select > Modify > Contract and choose a Contract By value of 10 pixels.

The selection has now contracted.

5. Press the DELETE key to delete the center.

6. CTRL/CMD-click on the layer thumbnail to select the entire ring.

7. Select the Gradient tool, set it for a linear gradient and choose the copper gradient preset.

8. Drag the gradient across the ring to make it appear more metallic.

9. Let's add some depth to the ring. Add a bevel as shown. Pay special attention to the gloss contour, depth and size sliders. Getting just the right balance between these three is the secret to great looking bevels.

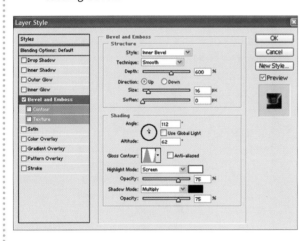

Here's the ring with the bevel:

10. A magnifying glass is not too much use without a handle. Let's make a simple one. Create a new layer and name it 'handle'.

11. Draw a rectangle with the Rectangular Marquee tool.

12. Using the same gradient, fill the rectangle and produce a cylinder.

13. Drag the handle into position and rotate it using the Free Transform tool (CTRL/CMD+T).

The key to successful image development is the ability to think ahead. I think being a chess player helps me in Photoshop – you always have to be thinking several steps ahead in order to make the right combination of moves.

We'll need a **drop shadow** on the magnifying glass at some point. But if we were to just add a layer style, when we distort the background the drop shadow wouldn't distort.

We'll plan ahead:

1. Make the magnifying glass one object.
2. Create the drop shadow on a separate layer.
3. Isolate the section of the shadow to be distorted.
4. Merge the section of the shadow with the section of the background to be distorted.
5. Distort the area of background inside the lens including the shadow.

OK, time for the walk through.

14. Link the handle and ring layers together.

15. Click the arrow at the top right and choose Merge Linked. The magnifying glass is now one object. The reason we have done this is so that we can create a single drop shadow.

16. Duplicate the handle layer and select the bottom one.

17. Ctrl/Cmd-click the handle layer to load the selection and fill the bottom magnifying glass with black.

18. Deselect and move the shadow down and to the left.

19. Soften the shadow with a Gaussian Blur (Filter > Blur > Gaussian Blur).

20. Drop the opacity of the layer down to 68%.

We now have a magnifying glass frame with a drop shadow. Right now it looks like there is no glass in the lens – we'll correct that now.

Creating the lens

1. Link the magnifying glass and the shadow. Place the glass right where you want the background to show through the lens.

2. Select the handle copy layer. Using the Magic Wand tool, make sure 'use all layers' is deselected, and select the space in the center of the lens.

3. We now need to make a copy of the background inside the lens. Choose the background layer and press Ctrl/Cmd+J to copy the selection to a new layer. Name this 'Layer 1' if it isn't already.

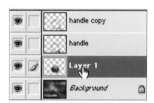

4. Now to separate the shadow inside the lens from the rest of the shadow. Load the circular selection again. The quickest way to do this is to Ctrl/Cmd-click on Layer 1. Then select the handle layer.

5. Press Ctrl/Cmd+Shift+J to cut the selection to a new layer (Layer > New > Layer via Cut). This will separate the shadow to two layers. Name this new layer 'shadow in glass'.

6. Link the shadow in glass layer with the copied background layer, Layer 1. Go to 'Merge linked' again. Now the shadow and the background sections are ready to be distorted together.

7. With the shadow in glass layer active, load the selection.

8. Go to Filter > Distort > Spherize and choose 75%.

9. Click OK and see the distortion in the lens. Let's take this effect further. How about the intensified light that shines through a magnifying glass? Keep the selection active.

Now go to Filter > Render > Lens Flare and choose the settings as shown in the screenshot:

10. Click OK and don't touch anything yet.

11. Choose Edit > Fade Lens Flare. The reason I said don't touch anything is because the fade option is only available immediately after applying a filter. Once you have done anything else this option is no longer available. What we want to do here is just apply the light effect of the lens flare without the color effect.

12. In the 'Fade' dialog box, change the mode to Luminosity and click OK.

Now you can see our lighting effect. Notice the lens is beginning to take shape. All it needs now is some glass reflections.

13. With the selection still active, create a new layer and name it 'reflection'.

Set white as the foreground color and choose the Gradient tool. Use the following settings for a 'Foreground to Transparent' gradient:

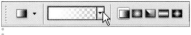

14. Drag the Gradient tool from the bottom of the lens up about a third of the way up. Deselect.

15. Let's add depth to our reflection. Press CTRL/CMD+T for the Free Transform tool. Holding down the SHIFT key (to constrain proportions) and the ALT/OPTION key (to scale from center), drag one of the corners in a little bit to shrink the reflection slightly. Apply the transformation.

16. Next, apply a Gaussian Blur to soften the edges. Use between 2-3 pixels.

17. Choose Free Transform again and rotate the reflection around the lens a bit. Apply the transformation and lower the opacity to suit your tastes.

18. Duplicate the reflection layer and use Free Transform once more to reposition the copy on the top of the lens.

19. Apply the transformation and you're done. Here is the image with the magnifying glass showing the distortion:

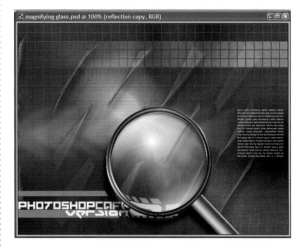

This is what it looks like on another image. Just link the magnifying glass layer, drop shadow and reflection layers, and then drag them to a new image. Make a selection around the lens, copy a section of the background, distort it and you have replicated the magnifying glass effect!

2: Water and liquid metal drops

This tutorial is a progressive tutorial. A lot of the steps are the same for the water and the metal. This tutorial is unique in that we will follow a path and then split it near the end and produce both water and metal drops. We'll then step out a little bit and turn the water into blood.

1. Start with any image in the RGB color space. I have provided a modified version of one of my wallpapers here, `Wetter the better.psd`.

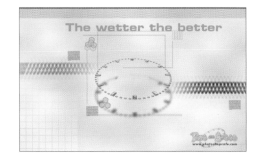

2. Create a new layer. Reset the fore and background colors (by pressing D) and create some clouds using Filter > Render > Clouds.

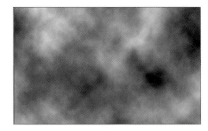

3. Go to Filter > Stylize > Find Edges.

4. Adjust the levels to make the texture stand out more (Image > Adjustments > Level or CTRL/CMD+L). Drag the left slider to the right, until it is lined up with the start of the "peak" on the histogram.

The histogram is what the black "mountain" is called – it represents the tonal distribution of the image.

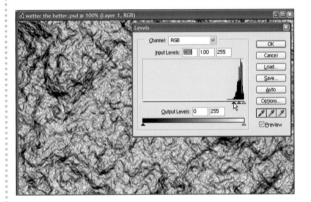

5. Let's isolate the shape of the drops now: Filter > Sketch > Plaster.

6. Let's make some adjustments in the plaster controls. Move the 'Smoothness' to maximum. Adjust the 'Image Balance' until you see the drops begin to separate from the background. Don't do it too much so that they are all tiny drops though, we'll want a bit of substance for this effect. Click OK.

You should see something like this. If it looks inverted, skip the next step.

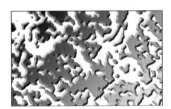

7. Invert the image.

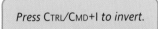

Press CTRL/CMD+I to invert.

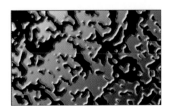

8. Run an 'Unsharp Mask' to tighten up the edges (Filter > Sharpen > Unsharp Mask). Keep the Radius low and the Amount high. Play with the Threshold until you have a satisfactory result. Click OK.

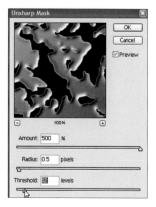

9. We now want to isolate the background. Choose the Magic Wand tool, with a tolerance of 2. There are 256 levels of gray – the tolerance will determine how many levels outside the exact sampled shade the Magic Wand will select. Make sure that 'Contiguous' is unselected. Contiguous will limit the selection to adjacent pixels. Without this option all similar colored pixels will be selected across the entire image with a tolerance of only 2 shades of gray.

10. Click on the black to select it.

11. Press the DELETE key to delete all the black and reveal the background beneath.

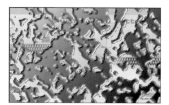

Liquid metal

This is where the tutorial will split. We'll create the molten metal first.

1. Save the image now.

2. Duplicate the water layer and name it 'metal'. Hide the water layer and make the metal layer active.

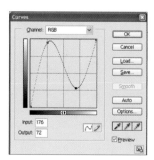

3. Let's enhance the metal look. Go to Image > Adjustments > Curves. Create a kind of 90 degrees inverted "S" in the curves dialog box. Press OK.

4. For best results, run curves again and choose a similar setting. This should really make our metal shine.

> *Don't try the curves a third time. It seems that after two applications the effect begins to break down and become too complex to appear real.*

5. Click OK.

See how shiny the metal is now.

6. Apply a soft drop shadow to enhance the effect.

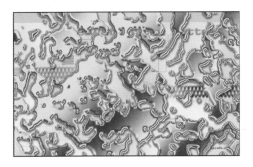

Water Drops

Let's leave the metal now and create the water.

1. Hide the metal layer. Reveal the water layer and make it active.

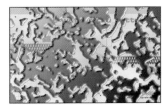

2. Change to 'Overlay' mode to give a more transparent appearance.

This is the result. It looks like water sure enough, but if we distort the background, the results will be much more convincing.

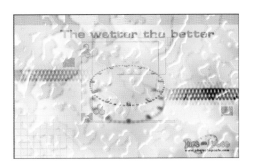

3. Load the selection of layer water by CTRL/CMD-clicking on the layer thumbnail.

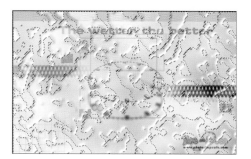

This effect can be used on windows looking out into a rainy days, or surfaces covered in liquid or lots of variations, use your imagination.

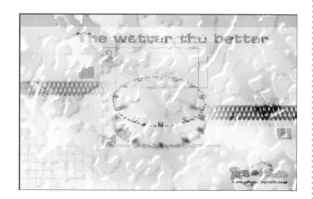

4. Choose the background and press CTRL/CMD+J to copy the selected portion of the background to a new layer. Name the layer 'distortion'.

Blood

If you are feeling daring, let's convert this water to blood.

5. Load the selection on the distortion layer. Now go to Filter > Distort > Ripple. We've used a setting of 156 here.

1. Turn on the metal layer and change the Blending Mode to 'Hard Light' and the opacity to 53%.

Notice how much better the result is now. Pay special attention to the way the text distorts.

2. Select the water layer.

3. Go to Image > Adjustments > Hue/Saturation. To add the red color check 'Colorize', crank the 'Saturation' all the way up and move the 'Hue' until you see a bright red. Finally lower the 'Lightness' slider until we get a nice deep red color. Click OK.

Change the blending mode from overlay to 'Multiply' mode – this will add more "substance" to our effect.

If you are having trouble producing a good red color, try changing to 'Multiply' mode before using the hue/saturation.

And there you have the blood effect!

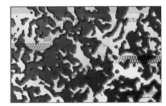

An optional step to make the blood more reflective is to also show the metal layer, change it to multiply mode and 72% opacity.

Here is the result, in some cases this will look better and others it won't, this depends on the background and desired result. Experiment and try changing some of the settings to see what you come up with. Especially experiment with blending modes and opacity of different layers.

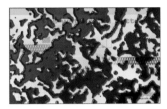

Here is an image that I applied this water technique to:

In this chapter you have learned about transparency and how it interacts with its surroundings. You've learned how to distort backgrounds to match the curves of the lenses. You have also learned how to add color in a translucent way instead of just flat color. Using this technique, you will add a lot of realism to your images. You can now create images with more depth and the appearance of "another dimension."

Try these techniques to add a bit of interest to products shots, or ads. Imagine what you could do to a brochure for an aquarium or a magazine ad for a scuba diving product. You could even just go crazy and create a totally surrealistic image just for fun or to attract attention to your design.

Chapter 15
Collaging Secrets

This chapter contains many tips and secret methods to creating great looking collages and backgrounds. These types of images are more popular than they have ever been. Imagine being able to create dynamic collages and backgrounds to be used in your design, web and multimedia projects. The ability to create eye-catching collages will add a lot to your skills and portfolio.

Blending images

I wish I had a dollar for every time I've been asked how to blend two images together. This tutorial will demonstrate how to blend two images with the gradient mask. Then we'll take it further and take total control of the masks.

1. Open `world.jpg` from the CD. (You can use any image in RGB mode for this background.)

2. Open `bike sprocket 5.psd` from the CD and drag it into the main image.

3. Resize the sprocket image to fit, using CTRL/CMD+T and holding down SHIFT while resizing to keep its proportions the same.

4. Click the 'Add layer mask' icon at the bottom of the Layers palette.

5. Reset the palette colors to default by hitting D on your keyboard and choose the Gradient tool.

6. In the options toolbar, choose 'foreground to background' and 'linear'.

7. Drag the Gradient tool across the image, ensuring that you're in the layer mask and not painting on the image.

8. Notice how the image smoothly blends to transparent. I will now explain how this works and offer a couple of steps to further illustrate this to you. Solid understanding and control of layer masks is paramount in good collage design.

When a new mask is applied to an image it doesn't seem to have any effect initially

What's happening is this – imagine that the layer is a picture projected on the wall like, say, a slide. As long as there is nothing blocking the path of the light, the picture will be displayed. All of a sudden, someone jumps up in front of you and begins to make animal hands on the screen. The hand is blocking the light and therefore casting a black shape on the screen, which is really an absence of light.

Layer masks are like the hands in front of the projector. Except, where a mask is blocked it will not show a black shadow, instead, it will hide the layer's contents and reveal whatever is underneath that layer. Also, the mask is not simply either on or off, it can show 256 levels of transparency. Each level of transparency is controlled by a level of gray applied to the mask.

When a mask is applied to a layer, by default it's filled with white. White has no effect on the layer. However, black would make the layer totally transparent. Needless to say that each level of gray will produce a different degree of transparency. 50% gray would produce 50% transparency.

Now look at the gradient we just made. Notice the mask has a grayscale gradient, which matches the faded blend on the layer. You can also selectively paint away or restore parts of the layer by using a brush on the layer mask.

9. Let's restore part of the image. Choose a soft brush of 100px and make white the foreground color. Remember that white will make the layer 100% opaque (provided we're painting at 100%).

10. Select the layer mask and paint with the white brush. See the image begin to return?

11. Now swap the foreground color for black (hit X). We'll now demonstrate the opposite effect.

12. Paint in the bottom part of the sprocket and notice the image begin to fade.

All right! Hopefully you have a better understanding of layer masks now. Let's continue with the collage.

13. Open `cyclist 8.psd` from the CD. (Both this picture and the sprocket are from Hemera Images)

14. Drag the image of the cyclist into the main picture and resize to suit your tastes.

Notice how the sprocket is now competing with the cyclist image. Let's make the composition balance a bit more.

15. Lower the opacity of the sprocket layer to 73%.

Notice how the sprocket is now blended back and yields its attention to the cyclist who is really the main focus of this design.

Color is very useful, not just as a communication tool, but also to bring together different elements and make them fit together tightly. A good example is the popular use of monotone collage images. I'll show you how to do this in one easy step, and then we'll selectively colorize a portion of the collage to bring attention to it.

16. At the bottom of the Layers palette is the 'Create new fill or adjustment layer' icon. Click on this and choose Hue/Saturation.

17. You'll now see a dialog box like this. Click Colorize and you notice that everything turns to one color immediately.

18. Adjust the Hue to move to other colors. Use the Saturation slider to add stronger color or to subdue it. I think you can figure out the Lightness on your own.

Here is our collage with the Hue/Saturation adjustment layer. It now looks like it all belongs together:

19. I said earlier that I'd show you how to selectively colorize. We'll colorize the bicycle only. Notice that the adjustment layer comes with its own layer mask as a standard feature. Well, this mask works exactly like a regular layer mask, except this time we're not fading an image, but an effect. Click on the mask.

20. Choose a black brush. Begin to paint and notice that the color begins to come back. Wait! Don't paint the entire bike in yet. Can you think of an easier way? Remember the bicycle was a clipped image and therefore it has transparency. Have you figured it out yet?

21. CTRL/CMD-click on the bike layer to load its transparency mask.

22. Now you can paint the bike back in easily without having to worry about going over the lines.

> If you're having trouble with this step, make sure that you're still painting on the layer mask of the adjustment layer.

23. Add some type and this could be the cover of a brochure.

24. Here's an extra little tip. At anytime (even after you've closed and reopened the file) double-click the adjustment layer and the 'Hue/Saturation' dialog box will pop up. Move the Hue slider for a quick color change.

We now have the same image in blue. You could show your client or boss two versions of the composition. Little do they know that it only took a few seconds to produce this variation, unless they read this book too!

Grunge effects

One of the hottest things out right now is the grunge brush effect. This is partly due to the fact that digital images are too perfect and people have been looking for ways to make them more down to earth and natural looking. I'll show you how to create your own brushes and enhance (or should that be 'dehance'?) your images.

1. Create a new document (this is where we'll create our brush). Make it 60 x 60 pixels at 72ppi with a white background.

2. Choose black as your foreground color and dab a few dots with a hard-edged brush. I would use from 10-15 pixels in size.

3. Apply a glass filter to it by selecting Filter > Distort > Glass... Play around with the settings – there are no rules here. Each brush should be unique.

4. Choose the Smudge tool and smudge the edges just a little bit, don't overdo it.

5. Make a selection around a portion of the image, using the Rectangular Marquee tool.

6. Drag it away to break it up a bit, using the Move tool.

   You can press the V key for the Move tool. Then use the arrow keys on the keyboard to nudge the selected portion of the image.

7. Do some more smudging to smoothen up some of the hard edges.

8. Go to Filter > Sharpen > Unsharp Mask... Now sharpen it to death, by pushing the amount all the way to 500.

9. Here's your final image or something like it:

10. Let's turn it into a brush. Select the entire image (CTRL/CMD+A).

11. Go to Edit > Define Brush. You'll now see a preview asking you to name the brush. Name it 'grunge brush'. Click OK and it's now added to your brush library.

12. Now let's use our new brush. Create a new document and add some text. Here I used the Impact font.

13. Rasterize the text by right clicking on the layer name and choosing Rasterize Layer from the menu – this is so that we can modify its pixels.

14. Choose the Eraser tool. Open the brushes palette and choose the new grunge brush that we just made.

You'll now see a preview of the brush shape over your image:

15. Dab all over the image to make it appear broken up. Remember that you can adjust the brush size. Dab with a variety of sizes. Be careful not to overdo it.

The trick is to dab with the brush and avoid dragging it.

16. Now drop the opacity down to 50% on the Brush options bar.

17. Apply the eraser to the text again, this time using a larger size.

18. Notice how the text looks over a different background:

The technique is not limited to text. Use it on images and shapes. This technique works excellently on photographic edges too. Hopefully this effect gives you some good ideas of how to make your work look a bit more artistic.

Design Project I

In the previous book, the design projects were very popular. However, I knew that these could have been better if Al and I were sitting in the same room when we wrote them. So I got on a plane and flew to Montana. Currently, I am sitting in Al's office in Montana. It's exciting to see what is coming out of this.

I am going to kick this one off by creating a shape, well a shell, of an interface. We're going to pass it back and forth on a zip drive and see what comes out. As an added feature this time, we thought of saving each round as a PSD and putting it on the CD so that you can jump in at any time and put your own twist on the co-op project.

1: Creating a shape

1. Let's begin with a new document, making use of the preset sizes in Photoshop 7. Choose '800x600' and 'RGB Color' mode. I always work in RGB over CMYK mode because the file size is smaller, all the filters will work and the color gamut is larger (more vivid colors). Choose 'Transparent' for the contents; this will create a new document with no background.

We're now going to use the Pen tool to draw a shape. The Pen tool is the best option because it draws the cleanest paths in Photoshop. The paths are drawn in vector format, which ensures a level of flexibility and scalability that is not possible with pixels.

2. To draw a vector shape, choose the Pen tool from the toolbox. In the Options bar, select 'Shape layers', the first option on the left. This will create a filled path that will be turned into a vector shape. The second option would create just a path.

The Pen tool may seem a little daunting at first, but gets easier with practice. If you are going to master Photoshop you have to learn the Pen tool at some point. For Illustrator users, the Pen tool in Photoshop performs exactly the same way.

Let's take a quick look at Bezier curves, which are created by the Pen tool. There are three elements you need to be aware of:

- **Anchor points**. These are the points that you add to your drawing; these are the dots used in "join the dots". Actually we just draw the dots and Photoshop will join them for us.

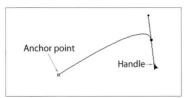

Anchor point

Handle

- **Handles**. These are the line segments that extend beyond the dots. These are how we control the way the dots are joined. They can be set to make a curve between the points or straight lines.
- **Closing points**. When we want to close a path, a small circle will appear when the mouse hovers over the start/finish anchor point.

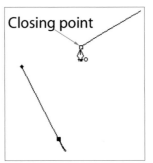

Closing point

There are two ways to draw. If you just click and them click elsewhere a straight line will be drawn between the two points. If you click and drag, an adjustment handle will appear indicating that you are now creating a curve. The curve will be created with the radius and direction of the drag.

3. Enough of the theory, let's actually do it now. (Don't forget, you can open the finished shape from the CD, it's called `shape1.psd`.) There are many methods to produce the result we are looking for; I've chosen the following method because it's the quickest way with the least steps to produce an abstract shape for our intended purposes. Click and drag downwards; notice the handle begins to appear:

4. Move your cursor to the right, and click and drag downwards again. Notice that you've created a curved section, and that as you drag you'll see the curve increase. Experiment with different lengths and angles, and try dragging up and down before you release the mouse button. In a normal path, you could select each of these handles and adjust the shape after you've completed the path. You can also move the anchor points later.

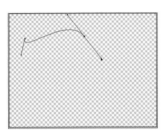

5. Click a third time. You will see a filled region now because we have more than two points. Note: the fill will always be the selected foreground color. If we had chosen the second option on the top toolbar, you wouldn't see a filled region.

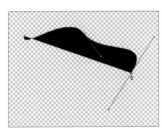

6. Keep clicking around the page perimeter until you have completed our rough shape.

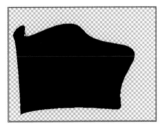

7. Once the path is complete you'll be left with a **shape layer**. A shape layer is somewhat like a type layer in that it has very limited flexibility. Just like we have rasterized text layers, and converted them to regular layers, we will now Rasterize the shape layer.

8. Create a new layer and link the new layer with the shape layer. Choose **Merge Linked** from the fly out menu at the top right of the Layers palette.

9. You'll now be able to make selections, trim and add to the shape. Using the Rectangular Marquee tool, make a selection across the top of the shape, then press the DELETE key to trim the shape.

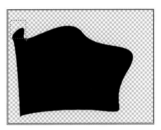

10. How about an area for a screen in our interface? Use the Rectangular Marquee tool again and draw a selection.

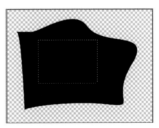

11. Press the DELETE key to cut out the screen. Next, choose the Elliptical Marquee tool and cut out a circle so we can add another component later.

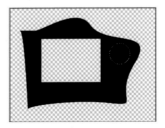

12. Keep trimming with the marquee tools. Also, use the Polygonal Lasso tool to draw irregular shapes.

> *The arrow keys on the keyboard can be used to nudge the selection without moving the image's pixels.*

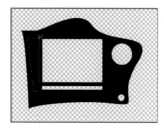

13. Finally we have our shape. Lots of holes and shapes will give us great flexibility to add gadgets to our interface.

Adding 3D depth to our shape

1. CTRL/CMD-click on the layer thumbnail. This loads the selection of our layer.

2. We're now going to create an Alpha channel and copy our shape into it. From there we can use this as a base to add depth to our image. Open the Channels palette and click the 'Create new channel' icon. The new channel will be called 'Alpha 1'. Click on the Alpha 1 channel. Don't deselect yet.

> *You'll have noticed that there is already a channel called 'Shape 1 Mask'. This is because we're using a shape layer. We could just skip a few steps and use this channel. However, we'll continue so that you know the procedure for times when you're not using a shape layer and want to produce the same result.*

3. The content of the Alpha channel is now displayed in the image window. You should see the marching ants selections around the shape. If you accidentally deselected you can just choose Select > Reselect or reselect your shapes using the Magic Wand tool, set to a low tolerance with the Contiguous box checked.

> *Hit CTRL/CMD-BACKSPACE to fill a selection with the background color.*

4. Fill the selection with white.

5. Don't deselect yet. We're currently creating a 'map' just like I showed you in the 3D chapter. Filter > Blur > Gaussian Blur. Use a setting of 7.5.

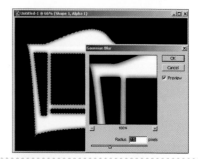

6. Our map is now ready for use. Click on the RGB channel in the Channels palette. This restores the display to the default composite display.

7. Return to the Layers palette. Create a new layer and name it 'shape'. Hide the Shape 1 layer.

8. If you deselected, load the selection by CTRL/CMD-clicking the shape layer and fill with a light gray color. Deselect.

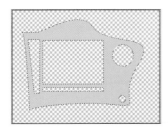

9. Time to make it look 3D: Filter > Render > Lighting Effects. Choose Alpha 1 from the texture channel.

10. Drag the four light control points to change the angle and width of the light. Adjust it so that the lighting is evenly spread out on the shape and not too bright or dark.

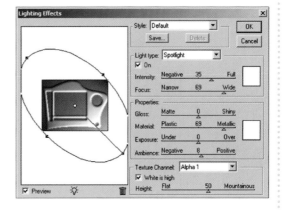

11. We want to create a colored light. Click on the color thumbnail.

12. Up pops the color picker. Choose a light brown/orange color. Press OK.

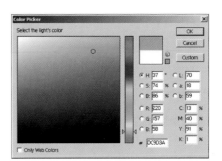

13. Your preview will now be colored with the hue that you chose from the color picker. When you are satisfied your settings are correct press OK.

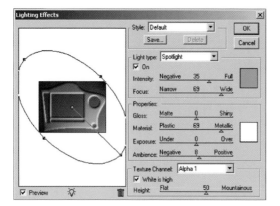

Almost instantly, your effect is applied to your layer. I still get a kick out of the way this filter adds so much depth to a shape. At this point, I'm going to pass the shape over to Al and see what he does with it.

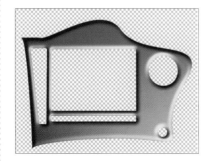

2: Altering the interface color

We have a good foundation for something... though neither of us is quite certain as of yet what will come of this. Looking at the shape, it appears to be some sort of interface, so that gives us a lot to go on really. Now, what type of interface will it be?

For this round, I'm going to start by adding some character and variation to the hues on the faceplate.

1. Select the shape layer.

2. CTRL/CMD-click the shape layer in the Layers palette to generate a selection of the shape.

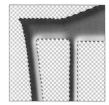

3. Click the 'Create a new layer' icon on the bottom of the Layers palette. A new layer named Layer 1 will be created just above the shape layer.

4. In the toolbox, select the Gradient tool. Set the following attributes for a copper gradient in the options bar. Note that the Mode has been set to **Difference**; this will have a big impact on the effect.

5. Fill the selection in the new layer with the gradient three times, each time coming from a different direction. The aim is for the gradient to be as rich and non-uniform as possible. On the third pass the majority of the layer will be primarily copper toned still, with a few other color variations in blue and violet.

6. That looks interesting, but I don't want to totally cover all of Colin's hard work. Hit CTRL/CMD+SHIFT+U to desaturate the layer, removing the color.

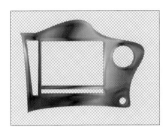

7. Go to Image > Adjustments > Curves. Create a three-point wave curve, as seen in the example below:

8. Before you click OK, you may want to save the curve. Click Save, name the curve (in this case I've named it `Difference Metal.acv`) and click Save again. Find a folder to keep it in the Photoshop directory, or where ever you store add-ons you've created. Once done, click OK in the Curves dialog box to apply the curve to the layer.

9. In the Layers palette, change the Blending Mode for Layer 1 to 'Difference'. Set the Opacity at 75%.

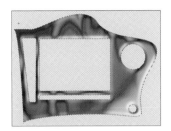

10. Go to Filter > Noise > Add Noise.... Set the Amount to 23% and choose the options Gaussian and Monochromatic.

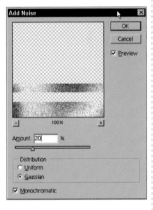

11. Go to Filter > Blur > Motion Blur. Enter the following settings in the 'Motion Blur' dialog box:

   ▪ Angle: 0 degrees
   ▪ Distance: 50 pixels

12. Go to Filter > Render > Lighting Effects. Enter the following settings in the Lighting Effects dialog box:

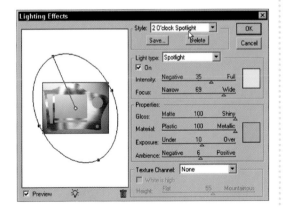

13. Here is a cool trick for adding recessed areas to the faceplate. Since the layer we are working with has a Motion blur applied to it, a bevel will create distorted recessed areas with the right settings. Click the 'Add a layer style' icon on the bottom of the Layers palette. Select Bevel and Emboss from the menu.

14. Enter the following settings for the bevel in the 'Layer Style' dialog box:

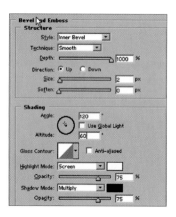

15. Click 'OK' to apply the layer style.

16. Hit CTRL/CMD+D to deselect.

That's it for this round! The interface now has a distorted bevel and brushed, heat-treated metal sheen to it. It will be interesting to see what my compadre does with this now.

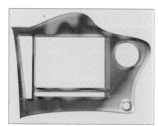

3: Adding an LCD display

Looks like Al has added to the bevel effect and created a worn look. I really like the texture in the body of the interface, but maybe the color needs some work. A military effect will be good.

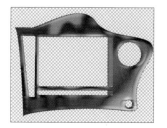

1. Choose the interface layer (layer 1) and make a selection. Add a Hue/Saturation Adjustment layer. Click on 'Create new fill or adjustment layer' icon in the Layers palette and choose Hue/Saturation.

2. Check Colorize and slide the Hue slider until we have a greenish hue.

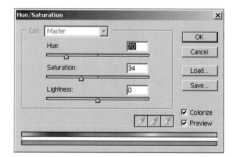

3. Press OK and we now have a more even colored interface shape. I'm going to now add an LCD screen before I pass it back to Al.

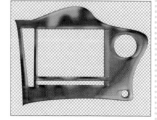

4. Create a new layer and name it 'screen'.

5. Choose the Magic Wand tool and change the options to reflect the screen capture. Choose 'Contiguous' so that only a single area will be selected and not all the similar colors on the whole image. Also choose 'Use All Layers' so that we can make our selection from any layer and not just the one with the object on it.

6. Click inside the screen area to make a selection of the blank area.

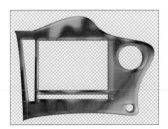

7. Choose a green/gray color for the foreground color. This is similar to the color found on most LCD displays.

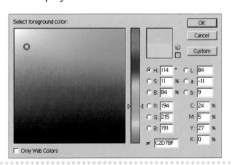

8. Fill the screen area with the new color by pressing ALT-BACKSPACE on the keyboard.

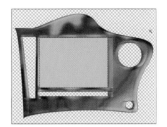

9. For a bit of added realism add some pixel noise: Filter > Noise > Add Noise. In this case, 3.48 will work fine. Choose 'Monochromatic', so that the noise isn't multi-colored.

10. Click 'OK' to add the noise to the layer. The base of the screen is now ready for some details.

Adding text

1. Choose the Type tool and drag it out in the shape of a rectangle. You will now see a bounding box. We're creating some paragraph text. The difference with paragraph text is that it will wrap to fit the box and create multi lines. Begin to type some characters into the text box. It doesn't have to make any sense because it will be so small no one will be able to read it anyway. Choose a clean font like Futura or Arial. Make the font color a dark gray.

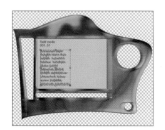

2. Select the text by clicking and dragging with the Type tool just like you would with a word processor. When the text is highlighted, make the font size 3.

3. The text should now be tiny. To increase the amount of text used, you can select and copy the text and then paste it to the end.

4. To adjust the size of the text box, use the Type tool and hover the mouse over the bounding box handle until it turns into a double-sided arrow. Click and drag to adjust the size.

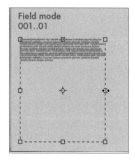

Here is our display with some heading text and a paragraph of tiny text added. This will simulate a computer readout.

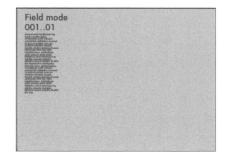

Adding a grid

1. Let's add a grid like we did in the collaging chapter. Create a new layer on top of the screen layer and name it 'grid'. Load the screen as a selection.

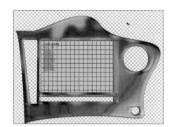

2. Fill and choose pattern, load the grid pattern from the patterns set 'colin.pat' on the CD, and the pattern will create the grid.

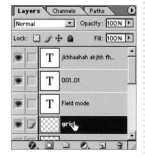

3. Lower the opacity of the grid to 12.

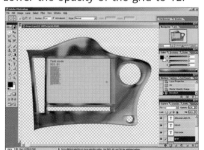

Adding some shapes

1. Why not add a few triangles to the screen to represent pointers? Create a new layer. Choose the Custom Shape tool and choose a triangle shape from the drop-down menu.

2. Select the third option from the left of the options bar, the 'Fill pixels' option. Draw a few triangles and place them around the screen.

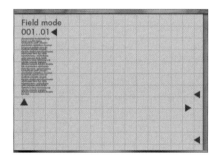

3. On the right hand side I have begun to draw a bar gauge. Choose the Line tool from the menu bar and a 1-pixel line to finish this gauge off.

4. Still using the Line tool, draw a line and then draw little tick increment marks across the line for the markers.

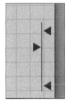

I think I have done enough on the screen for now, so it's back to you Al.

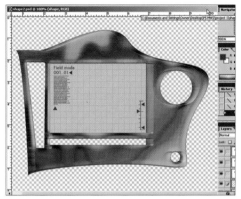

4: Creating a range finder

Interesting... I hadn't expected the interface to take a military twist. Now that the design seems to be taking a definite direction it presents a lot of ideas to continue the theme. A range finder view screen would fit into that open circular space, so let's get to work creating one.

1. Select the original shape layer. Now choose the Magic Wand tool and click the wand inside the empty space marking the circle to select the area.

2. For a military view screen, we need military colors. Click on the background color in the toolbox. Enter a color value of R:6, G:58 and B:2, or a numeric value of #063A02. For the foreground color enter a color value of R:7, G:236 and B:2, or a numeric value of #07EC02.

3. Now select the Gradient tool. In the Options bar, select the 'Foreground to Background' gradient, and then click in the gradient window to open the 'Gradient Editor'.

4. Move the background color stop (bottom right of the Gradient Editor) to the 40% location.

5. In the Options bar, set the following attributes for the gradient:

6. Starting in the center of the selection, draw the gradient to the border of the circle.

7. The gradient was placed on the shape layer; that needs to be corrected prior to moving on, as we will want to edit the screen separate from the other layers. Go to Layer > New > Layer via Cut (CTRL/CMD+SHIFT+J) to place the gradient screen on its own layer.

8. In the Layers palette, click the 'Create a new layer' icon.

9. Change the foreground color to a lighter green. Open the foreground color picker dialog box and enter values of R:144, G:253, and B:142, or a numeric value of #90FD8E.

10. Select the Elliptical Marquee tool and set the following attributes in the Options bar:

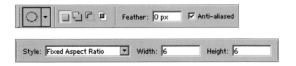

11. Make a circular selection on the range finder screen, nearly as large as the screen itself.

> *Remember to hold SHIFT to make a perfectly circular selection, and use the SPACEBAR to move the selection while you are still dragging it out.*

12. Go to Edit > Stroke…. And add a lime green stroke to the selection.

13. Click OK. Go to Select > Modify > Contract and contract the selection by 10 pixels. Then stroke again, repeating the process with a smaller selection this time. After

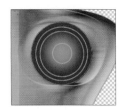

the third circle-stroke, hit CTRL/CMD+D to deselect. The screen should look like this example:

14. Select the Polygonal Lasso tool. Make a pie shaped selection on the outer two rings, as seen in the example below. Hit the DELETE key.

15. The process of adding cross hairs and blips to the screen is simple. First we'll make the crosshairs. Select the Pencil tool and set the following attributes in the Options bar:

- Brush: hard, 1 pixel
- Mode: Normal
- Opacity: 100%

16. Hold down the SHIFT key to keep the line straight and draw a vertical line through the screen. Then click the mouse on the left or right side of the screen to start a new line point. Again, hold down the SHIFT key and draw a line horizontally through the center of the screen.

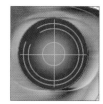

17. Now we will add a few blips. Go to the Options bar and increase the brush size to 3 pixels. Click the mouse over the screen a few times in different areas:

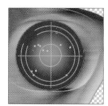

18. A compass pointer placed in the open area created in the outer rings adds more character to the screen. Select the Polygonal Lasso tool and make a triangular selection with one corner pointing toward the center of the display.

19. Fill the selection with the foreground color.

20. Go to Select > Deselect (CTRL/CMD+D).

21. In the Layers palette, change the Blending Mode for Layer 3 to 'Overlay'.

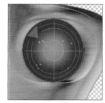

22. The screen needs something to hold it in place and keep moisture out of the circuitry. For this, we will create a metal ring surrounding the screen. CTRL/CMD+click Layer 2 to generate a selection the size of the screen.

23. Create a new layer just above Layer 2. This will be named Layer 4.

24. Go to Edit > Stroke. Enter the following settings in the 'Stroke' dialog box:

25. Name this layer 'Radar Ring'. Move it up the hierarchy in the Layers palette to just above the shape layer.

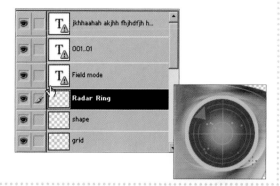

26. Click the 'Add a layer style' icon on the bottom of the Layers palette. Select Bevel and Emboss from the menu. Enter the following settings for the bevel in the 'Layer Style' dialog box:

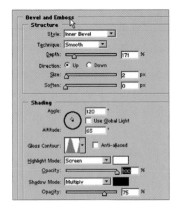

27. Select 'Contour' from the left hand menu of the 'Layer Style' dialog box. The default contour will work just fine for this example.

28. Select 'Gradient Overlay' and enter the following settings for a black to white gradient:

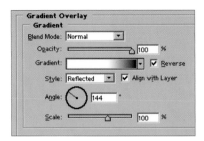

29. Click OK to apply the style. Now the ring is in place around the screen.

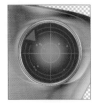

30. Let's go back and add a bit more detail to the screen. Select Layer 3 and hit CTRL/CMD+E to merge it with Layer 2 (the screen layer) directly below it. Rename the merged layer 'Radar Screen'.

31. Now create a new layer above the Radar Screen layer. Select the Type tool, and enter the following attributes in the Options bar:

32. Draw a text box in the new layer by click-dragging the mouse. Click within the box and enter a few lines of type... gibberish is fine. Hit ENTER when you have a few lines. Using the Move tool, place the text over the right side of the screen.

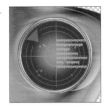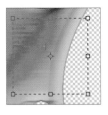

33. Right-click the type layer in the Layers palette and rasterize the layer.

34. Go to Edit > Transform > Scale and reduce the size of the text.

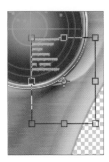

35. Position the text in the lower right quadrant of the screen.

There... the screen looks complete! Let's send it back to Colin and see what he comes up with next.

5: Adding a grip to the handle

1. Select the entire shape by using CTRL/CMD+click on the layer 1 (the main interface shape layer) thumbnail.

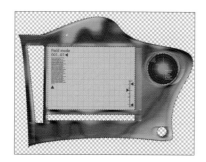

2. Choose the Lasso tool and 'Subtract from selection' on the Options bar.

3. Deselect all the selection except around the stem on the left. This is where we will make our grip.

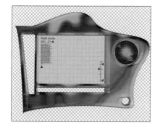

4. Now go to Select > Modify > Expand and choose 10 pixels. What we're doing is creating the outline for our grip.

Your selection should look like this:

5. Create a new layer and call it 'grip'.

6. Click on the Gradient tool and open the 'Gradient Editor'. Now construct a gradient that matches the one shown. This will be the foundation of our handle grip.

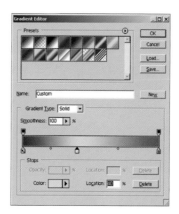

7. Click and drag the Gradient tool across the grip to apply the gradient.

Your grip should now resemble the screenshot here:

8. I think we ought to add a bit of texture to the grip. Click the 'Add a layer style' icon in the bottom of the Layers palette and move the softness slider up a bit to make a soft bevel. Choose 'Bevel and Emboss'. Keep the default settings except for moving the softness slider up a bit to make a soft bevel. Click on the words 'Texture' on the left-hand side of the dialog box. Click the black arrow on the right-hand side of the 'Pattern' window and open the scanline pattern.

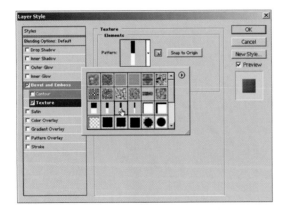

9. Use the 'Inner Shadow' effect to add some more depth to the grip and then click OK to apply the layer style.

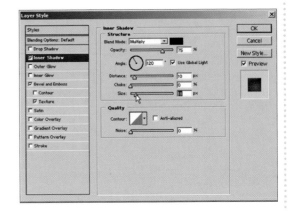

The handle has a bit more depth and texture now. Let's cut a couple of grooves into it.

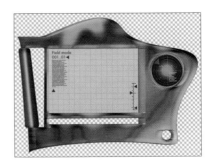

10. Using the Rectangular Marquee tool, make a thin selection near the bottom.

11. Press the DELETE key to remove that portion of the grip.

12. Do the same for the top section of the grip.

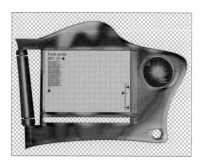

13. Lets add a row of buttons. Create a new layer and name it 'buttons'.

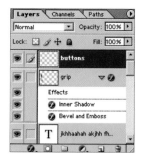

14. Select the Rounded Rectangle tool.

15. Set the radius to 10 pixels.

16. Click and drag to draw a new button.

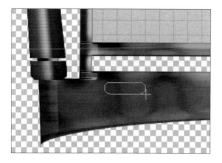

17. Press the ALT/OPTION key and click and drag out a copy of the button. Hold the SHIFT key to keep the baselines aligned. Drag out 3 more copies until we have a total of 5 buttons. Don't worry about evenly spacing them yet.

18. Let's distribute them evenly now. Link the five button layers together.

19. Click on the 'Distribute horizontal centers' button on the Options bar.

The buttons are evenly spaced now.

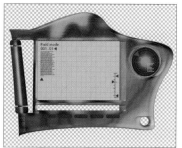

237

20. What is a screen without some kind of video display? Create a new layer and name it 'screen panel'.

21. Using the Rectangular Marquee tool, draw a rectangle around the area that we will use as a screen.

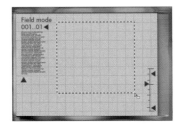

22. Fill with white.

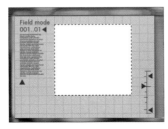

23. Let's make some digital static. Go to Filter > Noise > Add Noise. Use around 60% noise this time. Also use the uniform setting instead of the gaussian. This will give the noise a smoother appearance.

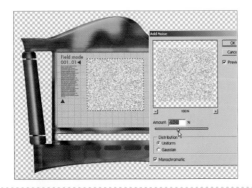

24. Here is a really cool trick to create digital noise. Press the SHIFT+BACKSPACE keys to open the 'Fill' dialog box. Choose pattern and scanline. Press OK.

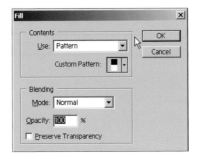

You'll now see a scanline right over the noise layer.

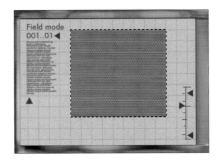

25. Click Edit > Fade. The 'Fade' dialog box is only available immediately after applying an effect. Change the setting to 'Overlay' mode.

26. You now have a really interesting noise effect. Drop the opacity to 61%.

You should now have what looks like a screen full of static. We'll add a picture to the screen.

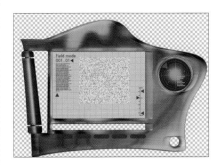

27. Open any picture you choose. I used the dunes image from the samples folder in the Photoshop installation directory.

28. Drag the image into our interface document. Resize it to the same size as the screen using the Free Transform tool Ctrl/Cmd+T.

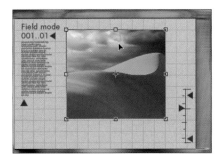

29. Drag the new image layer below the screen panel layer.

The image is now showing thorough the static.

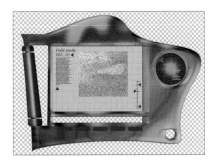

30. Before I pass the PSD back to Al I think we are in desperate need of some house cleaning. The layers palette is beginning to look cluttered. Create a new layer set and name it 'screen'.

31. Drag all the layers that make up the screen to the screen set.

> *Whenever you add a layer to a set it will automatically be added to the top of the stack. To keep all your images displaying correctly, begin with the bottom most layers when you drag them into the set.*

You can see the layers are indented to indicate that the set is expanded.

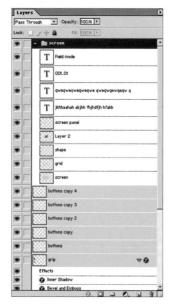

32. Click the folder icon to collapse the layer set and hide its contents.

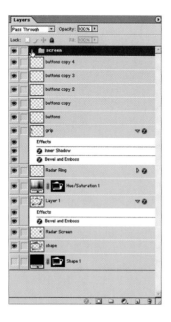

33. Create layer sets for the buttons, radar and iface. Drag the layers into the appropriate sets. There! That's how I like the Layers palette to look. This becomes very important when you are working with a lot of layers. For example, I made an image of a guitar and it contains over 300 layers. You can view it on my website at www.photoshopcafe.com.

6: Adding a speaker

I notice that Colin has placed the layers into sets to keep them organized. I must admit I'm horrible at doing that, so I'm glad that he thought of it. I may be allergic to organization, but it is still good policy.

There is a lot of open space left around the edges of the interface. How about adding a speaker for hearing the contact blips and receiving messages?

1. CTRL/CMD+click the shape layer, now found in the iface layer set. A selection of the interface shape will be generated. Go to Select > Modify > Contract. In the 'Contract Selection' dialog box, contract the selection by 32 pixels and click OK.

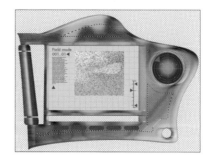

2. There are a few areas selected that we want to omit from the speaker-creating process. Select the Rectangular Marquee tool and set the following attributes in the Options bar:

3. Draw selections around all the areas you want to omit from the speaker area. When you are done, you should have only the area where the speaker is to be placed selected, in this case just beneath the radar screen.

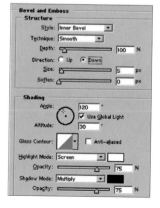

4. Hit CTRL/CMD+J to create a new 'Layer via Copy'. Rename the newly made copy layer 'Speaker Grid' in the Layers palette.

5. Click the 'Add a layer style' icon and choose Bevel and Emboss from the pop-up. Enter the following settings for the bevel:

6. Select the Rectangular Marquee again. Keep the previous settings, but change the selection type in the options bar to 'New Selection'.

7. Draw a narrow horizontal selection across the top tip of the new layer. Make sure the selection is more than the width of the speaker.

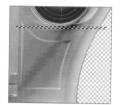

8. Hit the DELETE key.

9. Using the Move tool, move the selection down 10 pixels or so and hit DELETE again. Continue moving and deleting until lines are made through the entire speaker area.

10. Open the layer styles for the Speaker Grid layer again. Enter the following settings for the 'Inner Shadow':

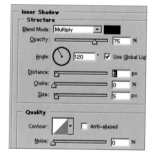

11. Now select 'Outer Glow' and enter the following settings:

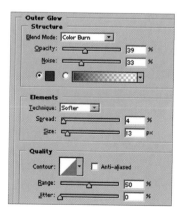

12. Now apply an 'Inner Glow' with a dark gray color and the following settings:

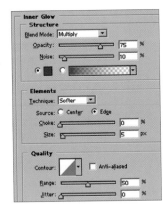

13. Enter the following settings for the 'Color Overlay':

14. Click OK to apply these new layer styles.

15. Now that we have the grill the speaker will be seen through, it's time to set up the speaker itself. Create a new layer above the 'Speaker Grid' layer.

16. We'll work on the speaker image in a separate document, so hit CTRL/CMD+N and make a 300 x 300 pixel document at 100 ppi, with a transparent background.

17. Use the Rectangular Marquee tool to make a narrow horizontal selection across the entire width of the image. Fill the selection with Black, 100%.

18. Using the Move tool, hold down the ALT key to drag out two copies of the filled selection. When you have three bars, go to CTRL/CMD+D to deselect.

19. Go to Filter > Distort > Polar Coordinates. Select 'Rectangular to Polar' and click OK.

20. Hit CTRL/CMD+A to select all, and then copy the selection (CTRL/CMD+C), before returning to the interface image.

21. Now paste (CTRL/CMD+V) the rings in the layer above the speaker grid layer. Use the Move tool to position them over the speaker grid.

22. Click CTRL/CMD+T to enter Free Transform mode, resize the speaker to fit over the grid. Hold down SHIFT to move the speaker while in Free Transform mode.

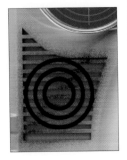

23. CTRL/CMD+click the speaker grid layer. Go to Select > Inverse and hit DELETE. The remainder of the rings will appear as though they can be seen through the speaker grid.

24. Select the Gradient tool. Load the PSW2-Metal-1.grd gradient set found on the CD and then set the following gradient options in the options bar:

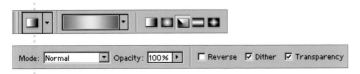

25. CTRL/CMD+click the rings layer to generate a selection. Starting in the center of the rings, draw the gradient to the outer ring. Set the Blending Mode for the rings layer to 'Difference'.

26. Create a layer set and drag all the speaker parts to this set. Rename the layer set to reflect its content, 'Speaker Parts'.

We're all set to receive audio! Now let's send it to Colin again for the next part.

7: Enhancing the glass and buttons

Love the speaker, what is multi-media without sound? I guess just media! What this interface really needs now is some highlights on the glass and some life to the buttons.

1. We'll tackle the buttons first. Open the buttons set and choose the first button.

2. Open the 'Layer Style' dialog box and apply a bevel. Change the Gloss Contour to give it a glassy appearance.

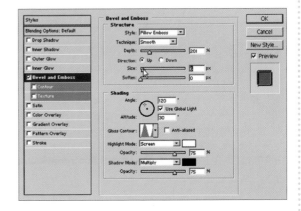

243

3. Select Color Overlay and apply a lime green color to the button.

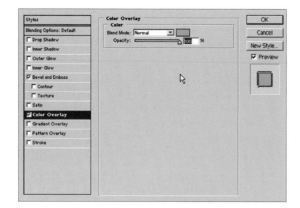

One of the buttons is now looking much better. We'll quickly apply this effect to the rest of the buttons in the row.

4. Right/CTRL-click on the layer style in the Layers palette and choose Copy Layer Style.

5. Make sure that the buttons are still linked. You should see the chain link icon. Now choose Paste Layer Style to Linked.

The same style is now attached to all the buttons.

6. Let's apply a button to the rounded hole in the bottom right. Use the Magic Wand tool and select 'Use all Layers' from the options bar. Click in the hole to select it.

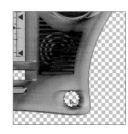

7. Create a new layer and name it 'round button'.

8. Click CTRL/CMD-BACKSPACE to fill with the background color, (in this case white). It doesn't matter what the color is as we will define it in the layer style. The layer has to have a fill for the layer style to work.

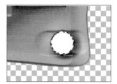

9. Right-click on the layer name and choose Paste Layer Style.

The bevel will now be applied to the button.

10. Let's change the color of the button without changing any of the other attributes. Double-click the 'Color Overlay' layer effect.

11. The 'Layer Style' dialog box will now open with the color overlay option open. Click the color picker and choose a red color.

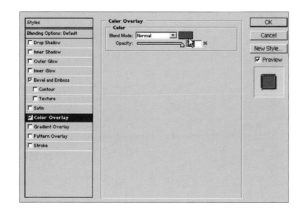

The button will now appear red. The buttons are looking pretty good now; let's tackle the glass highlights.

12. Create a new layer set and name it 'reflections'. Create two new layers and call them 'radar' and 'screen'. This is where we'll add the highlights.

13. CTRL/CMD+click on the radar screen layer to load the selection of the radar shape. Select the blank radar reflection layer.

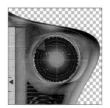

14. We're going to create highlights by using the Gradient tool. Choose the Gradient tool and use the foreground (white) to transparent linear option. Make sure the 'Transparency' option is checked.

15. Click and drag the gradient from the top to halfway down the screen. The screen is now looking like it has a glass lens on top of the display.

16. Let's add the highlights to the screen. Load the selection for the screen from the screen layer set. Click on the blank screen reflections layer.

17. Using the same gradient, drag diagonally from the top left to the bottom right of the screen.

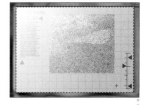

245

18. Using the Elliptical Marquee tool, draw a large oval, covering the bottom part of the screen.

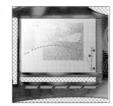

19. Press the DELETE key to delete the selection. Next, make another selection covering the right side of the screen.

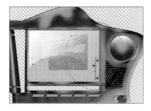

20. Press the DELETE key again.

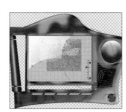

21. CTRL/CMD+T for the Free Transform mode. Shrink the selection so that it's slightly smaller than the edges of the screen. Press the ENTER key to apply the transformation and then deselect.

22. Softening the edges will add some depth to the reflection. Go to Filter > Blur > Gaussian Blur and use a setting of 1.3.

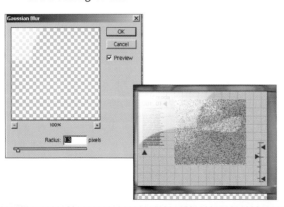

23. Duplicate the screen layer. This will produce a new layer called 'screen copy'.

24. Using the Free Transform, reflect the copy of the reflection and position it to the right.

25. We'll add one more reflection to the bottom of the screen. Create a new layer and name it 'bottom h-light'. Select the entire screen area.

26. Drag the Gradient tool from the bottom of the 'screen' to about a third of the way up.

27. Once again using the Free Transform, reduce the size of the gradient. This is a great method to make the edges of reflections look rounded. Apply the transformation and then Deselect before applying a 2 pixel Gaussian Blur.

28. Let's display the interface in a better way. We are going to add a drop shadow and this will stand out much better on a white background. Create a new layer and move it to the bottom of the layer stack and fill it with white. Next, choose the shape layer.

29. Apply a drop shadow to the entire shape. This adds the illusion of distance between the interface and the background. Increase the size setting to make the shadow appear softer.

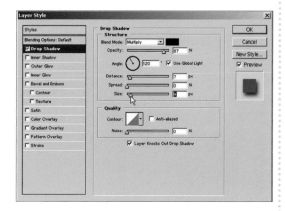

It's looking pretty good. However, the screen looks like it needs a drop shadow too for the appearance of depth.

30. Just click on the screen layer set and drag it behind the face layer set.

The drop shadow now has an effect on the screen.

Finally, before I send it back to Al, I've added some text to the buttons and also to the interface itself. What manufacturer wouldn't put a label on their product?

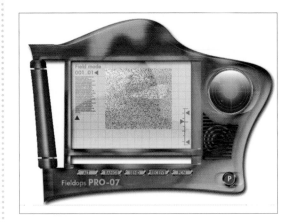

8: The bar

We're coming down to the wire now... only a few touch ups are really needed. First, we can deal with that open bar at the bottom of the interface, just below the view screen.

1. Open the iface layer set and select the shape layer.

2. Select the Magic Wand tool and click the wand inside the open area to generate a selection.

3. Create a new layer above the shape layer.

4. Select the Gradient tool and load in the `PSW2-Metall.grd` gradient. In the options bar, set the following attributes for the Gradient tool:

5. Starting at the top of the selection, draw the gradient down to the bottom of the selection.

6. The space has taken a metallic aspect due to the gradient used. However, we aren't really looking for a metal fill for the space. Go to Image > Adjustments > Brightness/Contrast. Enter the following settings in the 'Brightness/Contrast' dialog box:

    - Brightness: -100
    - Contrast: -38

7. Select the Rectangular Marquee tool and set the following attributes in the options bar:

Selection Type: Subtract from selection

    - Feather: 0 px
    - Style: Normal

8. Select the right third of the selected area with the marquee. This will subtract that area from the current selection.

9. Create a new layer just above the one filled with the gradient.

10. Change the foreground color to a bright red, and the background color to a darker red/brown.

11. Select the Gradient tool and set the following attributes for a 'Foreground to Background' gradient:

12. Starting from the right side of the selection, fill it with the gradient by dragging all the way to the left side of the selection.

13. In the Layers palette, change the Blending Mode for the layer to 'Vivid Light', and set the Opacity at 75%.

14. Select Layer 4 (this should be the layer filled with the bar gradient).

15. Open the layer styles for Layer 4 and select 'Drop Shadow' from the menu. Apply the default drop shadow settings.

16. Next, select 'Bevel and Emboss' from the left hand menu. Enter the following settings for the bevel:

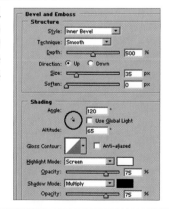

17. Select Layer 5 again (the one filled with the red gradient). We set the Blending Mode to 'Vivid Light' before, but that is a little harsh. Change the Blending Mode to Overlay, and increase the Opacity to 100%.

Now we have a status bar of some sort. I'm not sure of its function, but it looks good on the interface, so it must do something, right?

Creating an antenna

The last item I can think that this contraption needs is an antenna.

1. Create a new layer below all the layer sets.

2. Select the Rectangular Marquee tool. Use the previous settings, except change the selection type to 'New Selection'. Create a selection that appears to come from the top of the interface.

3. Select the Gradient tool and revert to the gradient we used earlier, PMW2-Metal1.grd.

4. Fill the selection from left to right with the gradient.

5. Now go to Image > Adjustments > Curves. Enter a curve similar to the one seen in the example screenshot. Click OK when the gradient has a metallic sheen to it. Don't worry if you have to use a slightly different curve to achieve the antenna gradient effect shown.

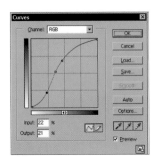

6. Create a new layer beneath the one you've just filled. Again, select the Rectangular Marquee and repeat the process used with the previous antenna piece, only narrower this time, placed behind the first and extending above it. Fill with the same gradient and apply the curve again.

7. One more time, create a new layer beneath the other two and repeat the process with a narrower selection. Hit CTRL/CMD+D to deselect.

8. Select the layer of the first antenna piece that you created. Click the 'Add a layer style' icon on the bottom of the Layers palette and select Stroke from the menu. Enter the following settings for the stroke (note the color is a dark gray/black):

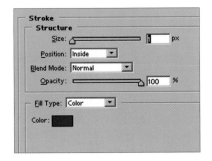

9. In the Layers palette click and drag the layer style setting you just applied to the other two antenna layers.

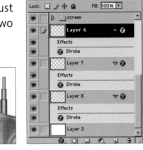

10. Now we just need to top it off. Create a new layer above the antenna layers.

11. Using the Elliptical Marquee tool create a small circular selection at the top of the antenna.

12. Hit the D key, and then the X key to place white in the foreground and black in the background.

13. Reselect the Gradient tool and set the following attributes for a 'Foreground to Background' gradient:

14. Starting in the upper left quadrant of the selection, draw the gradient down and to the right.

15. Starting with the ball you just made, hit CTRL/CMD+E and merge the antenna layers together. Rename the final layer 'Antennae'.

16. For the final touch, click the 'Add a layer style' icon on the bottom of the layers palette. Select Drop Shadow from the menu, and enter the following settings:

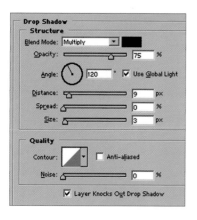

17. Click OK.

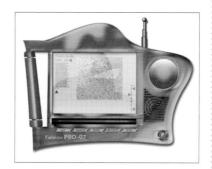

That's about it! Let's send it to Colin one more time for any finishing touches he would like to add.

9: Creating a vent

We're looking really good now. I don't think it needs much more. The only thing I can see is that the top section is looking a bit plain. I think we will add a vent to it and call it a finished project.

1. Select the Line tool for the toolbox and choose white as the foreground color. Make the 'Weight' 1 pixel.

2. Create a new layer and call it 'vents'. Draw a line across the top of the interface.

3. To make the line look recessed we'll duplicate it, invert it and move it 1 pixel. Duplicate the layer by dragging it to the 'Create a new layer' icon.

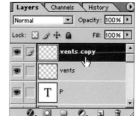

4. Press CTRL/CMD+I to invert the color of the new line. Press the up arrow on the keyboard once to nudge the line up by 1 pixel.

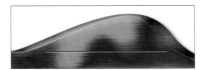

5. Link the vents and vents copy layer.

6. Select Merge Linked from the Layer menu. The recessed line is now on one layer.

7. Holding down the ALT/OPTION key, click and drag a copy of the line. Keep dragging until you have several lines in a row up to the top of the vent area.

8. Link all the vent layers.

9. Click the 'Distribute vertical centers' button from the options bar. This will evenly distribute all the lines.

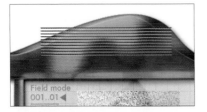

10. Now choose Layer > Merge Linked again.

11. Using the Polygonal Lasso tool, make a selection around the area that you want to delete.

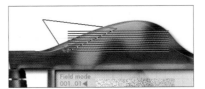

12. Press the DELETE key.

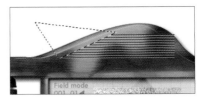

13. Make a selection around the other side of the vent.

14. Delete to trim the vent. Finally we have the finished project. Here is our interface/special military device.

As I mentioned earlier on you can open the examples from the CD and jump in at any point of the project and add your own twist to it, or just follow along. This has been a lot of fun creating the design and playing some Photoshop tennis with Al. It's amazing what you can come up with when you put your minds together on a project.

Design Project II

For the second design project, we decided to do a print job. A book cover seems like the order of the day, specifically a cover for this book. While the actual cover of the book will vary, it will be good for you to have a rare glimpse into the creative process and see how an image evolves and changes as it's shaped into something that we, the designers, feel happy about. You'll also learn a couple of things about the world of designing for print. Notice that some of the effects we apply will be changed later.

1. The first thing we need to do is create the new canvas. Eight by ten inches is a pretty standard size for magazines and coffee table books. The resolution must be 300ppi for print. The printing press requires a much higher resolution than a screen display. As such, the file size will be larger. The empty file will be 20 megabytes and quickly increase as we add layers. You'll want to optimize your computer to produce large files - here are a few tips:

   ■ You can never have too much RAM.
   ■ Clear the hard drive of unneeded files. The more free space you have, the better Photoshop will run because it uses the free space as 'temporary RAM', or what's known as the Scratch Disk.
   ■ Optimize your hard drive by running a defragmentation program. These are built into system tools if you're on a PC, or use Norton Speed disk on a Mac.
   ■ Crop your images to the size needed. Just because you can't see it, it doesn't mean it's not there.
   ■ Work in RGB mode and only convert to CMYK at the end – this will keep the file size approximately a quarter smaller.

2. Create some text. Here I used Futura Extra Black at a 50 point size. If you don't have Futura, Arial is very similar.

3. Now create the second line in a different font for impact. I also set this one at 50 points. The second font I used is a freeware font called Planet Kosmos available for download at www.themeworld.com/fonts/indexP5.shtml. I made the word "most" a mid-gray color to make it a bit more eye catching.

4. I decided to make the "2" very large, 242 pts. Contrast in type is a great attention grabber. I dragged the "2" under the smaller text to help readability.

5. I then added the author names. I copied the color scheme and the font from the title so that the design would have some unity. Even though the new text is smaller, at 33 pts, it still ties in with the existing text. A big mistake would be using a different italic font. The other font may use a different angle and as such, spoil the flow of lines on the page.

6. I've added a strip across the center of the page. I made a new layer for the strip. It's a good idea to put most things on their own layer for a project like this, it will give you more flexibility to change things later. This is where the images will be placed. I think we have a pretty good foundation for a clean layout. I'll now hand it over to Al.

As always, it looks like Colin has a good start on things. You know me though – I simply can't allow those fonts to go untouched. To start, let's dress up the biggest font on the page – the number "2"

7. CTRL/CMD-click the "2" layer to select the text.

8. Click the 'Add a layer style' icon for the "2" layer and select Drop Shadow... Enter the following drop shadow settings in the Layer Style dialog box:

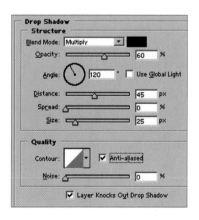

9. Select Inner Shadow from the left-hand menu. Enter the following settings for the inner shadow using an orange color:

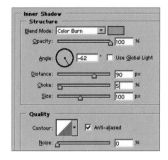

10. Select Bevel and Emboss. Enter the following settings for the bevel in the Layer Style dialog box:

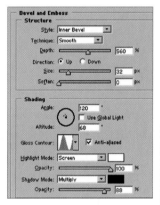

11. Select Contour from the left hand menu. Change the contour to the one named Gaussian, with Anti-aliased checked and the range set to 10%:

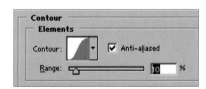

12. Select Satin from the menu on the left. Enter the following settings:

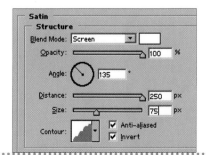

13. Select Gradient Overlay. Enter the following settings for the gradient overlay in the Layer Style dialog box. Use the black, white gradient found in the `project2.grd` set on the CD.

14. Select Pattern Overlay. Enter the following settings for the pattern overlay using the preset Satin pattern:

15. On the right side of the Layer Style dialog box, check the style icon. That looks pretty sharp, so save the layer style by hitting the New Style... button. Click OK.

I'm going to do something that irritates Colin – merge the layer to collapse the style. Create a new layer below the "2" layer.

16. Select the "2" layer and hit CTRL/CMD+E to merge it with the empty layer below it.

17. Go to Image > Adjustments > Brightness/Contrast Enter the following settings in the 'Brightness/Contrast' dialog box and click OK:

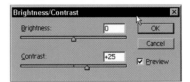

18. Use CTRL/CMD+D to deselect.

19. Select and move the "photoshop" and "mostwanted" text layers into position under the 2 as seen in the example.

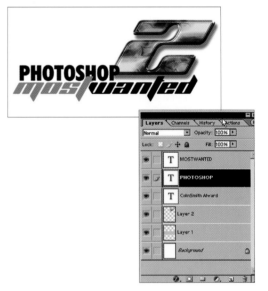

20. Now let's add an element from the book itself. Find and open `GlassGlobe2.psd` on the CD.

21. In the GlassGlobe2 image, click the eye next to the Background layer, the 'Floor' layer and the 'Base Sphere copy' layer to render them invisible. Select the Base Sphere layer and hit CTRL/CMD+SHIFT+E to merge all the remaining visible layers.

22. Drag the merged Base Sphere layer into the book cover image. Center the sphere over the gray strip – I just do this by eye, although you could use an align option if you find it easier.

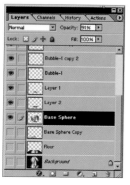

23. Go to Edit > Transform > Scale. Increase the size of the sphere so that it overlaps the top and bottom edges of the gray bar. Hit enter to accept the transform.

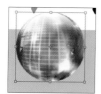

24. Go to Image > Adjustments > Hue/Saturation… Enter the following settings in the Hue/Saturation dialog box:

25. Click OK. I think that looks good for this round… back to you Colin!

Al has added an effect to the text and a sphere. I'm going to add some extra texture and color to the text.

26. Open up background.psd from the Design_Project_02 folder on the CD.

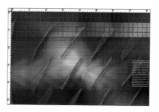

27. Drag it into our book cover document.

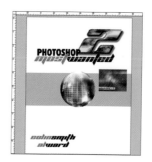

28. Reposition and resize the image until it completely covers the number 2.

29. Make a selection around the number 2 by CTRL/CMD-clicking on its layer thumbnail.

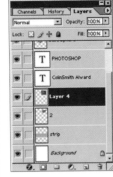

30. Make sure the texture layer is highlighted. Invert the selection by clicking CTRL/CMD+SHIFT+I. Press the DELETE key to trim the texture to the text.

31. Change the Blending Mode to Pin Light. Use CTRL/CMD+D to deselect.

32. The new texture adds a nice enhancement to the effect that Al already made.

33. Let's enhance the 'image strip' area. Open hi_tech.psd from the CD.

34. Press CTRL/CMD+A to select the entire document.

35. Go to Edit > Define Pattern... and click OK.

36. Make a selection around the gray strip in the book cover document by CTRL/CMD-clicking the gray strip layer thumbnail.

37. Create a new layer just above the gray strip layer.

38. Go to Edit > Fill... Use Pattern and open the pattern we just saved in the custom pattern window.

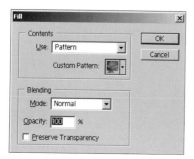

You'll now see our pattern tiled across the selected area.

39. We'll now add a blur effect and blend it with the regular tile. Duplicate the layer that has the pattern tile on it.

If the tiling doesn't appear exactly as shown here, move the selection to the top of the canvas, refill it with the pattern, and move it back into position. This works as the Pattern Fill always starts from the top left hand corner of the canvas.

40. If the strip area isn't still selected, load it now as a selection by CTRL/CMD-clicking on the layer thumbnail.

41. Go to Filter > Blur > Radial Blur... Choose Zoom and 100%.

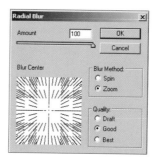

You should see this effect now. Remember that the layer underneath is unaffected by the blur. We're now going to blend it with the unaffected layer.

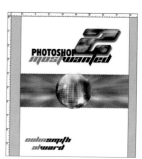

42. Add a layer mask to the blurred layer. Just click the 'Add layer mask' icon.

43. Choose a 500px soft brush and select black as the foreground color.

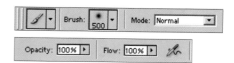

44. Begin to paint on the layer mask, just paint around the sphere in the center of the strip. You should end up with a nifty blended/blurred look as shown here. And now back to Al.

Hey, I really like what Colin did with the bar. I see he's altered my first pass somewhat, but that's the point to this project – getting input and alterations from two designers for a single work. Now the text I worked on before matches the background work Colin created.

45. There's still some type that has yet to be altered, and I just can't let that rest. Let's give some of the text a metal facelift. CTRL/CMD-click the Photoshop text layer to create a selection.

46. Create a new layer above the Photoshop text layer. Fill the selection with Black, 100% opacity.

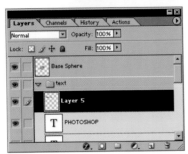

47. To preserve the integrity of the layers for the book cover layout, let's use a new image to apply metal to the text. Hit CTRL/CMD+C to copy the selection.

48. Hit CTRL/CMD+N to create a new document. Enter the following settings and click OK:

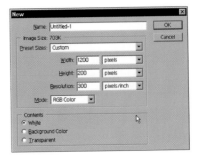

49. Hit CTRL/CMD+V to paste the type into the new document.

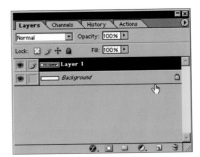

50. CTRL/CMD-click the pasted layer to generate a selection of the text.

51. The following process will produce really shiny metal. First, change the foreground color to R:153, G:153 and B:152, or #999998. Click OK.

52. Fill the selection with the foreground color.

53. Save the selection as a channel named ps-1, by going to Select > Save Selection and saving as a channel from the 'Save Selection' dialog box.

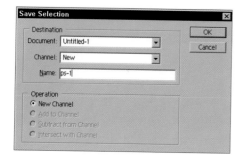

54. Hit CTRL/CMD+D to deselect.

55. In the Channels palette select the ps-1 channel.

56. Go to Filter > Blur > Gaussian Blur... Enter the following blur settings and click OK:

57. Go to Select > Reselect, then Select > Inverse, then Edit > Fill... using Black. Click OK.

58. Select the RGB channel.

59. Return to the Layers palette.

60. Use CTRL/CMD+D to deselect.

61. Go to Filter > Render > Lighting Effects... Enter the following settings, and be prepared to tweak them as results can vary. Then click OK:

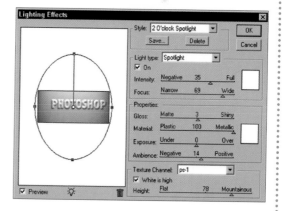

62. The image below shows the initial effect of the lighting applied to the text:

63. Go to Image > Adjustments > Curves… Enter a curve just like the one seen in the following example and click OK:

Now check the text:

64. Click the 'Create new fill or adjustment layer' icon, and select Levels from the menu. Select each channel individually and move the center slider to the left, as seen in the following examples:

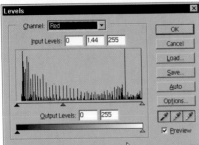

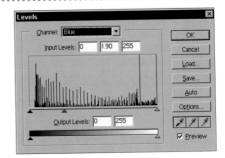

65. Once all three channels have been adjusted, click OK. The text should now have a blue reflective tint:

66. Hide the background layer by clicking the small eye next to it in the Layers palette.

67. Select the Adjustment layer. Hit CTRL/CMD+SHIFT+E to merge all the visible layers.

68. Drag and drop the text back into the book cover image. With the Move tool, place the text over the Photoshop layer and the fill layer. Move it up and to the left so the original text layers provide a drop shadow effect.

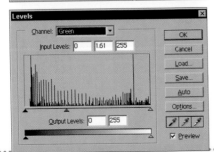

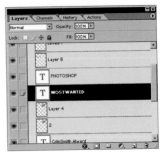

69. Select the Magic Wand tool. On the "mostwanted" layer, select the letters that spell out "wanted" with the Magic Wand tool. Hold down the SHIFT key while selecting the letters to add to each selection. When all the letters have been selected, repeat the process followed above to add the same metal effect to the "wanted" text.

It may look a little darker or lighter, but that's OK.

70. Select the Magic Wand tool again. Select the text that spells "most" on the "mostwanted" layer.

71. Create a new layer. Fill the selection with 50% gray, 100% opacity.

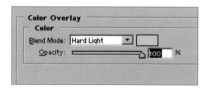

72. To contrast this text with the metal, let's build a quick layer style. On the bottom of the Layers palette, click the 'Add a layer style' icon. Select Color Overlay… from the menu. Enter the following settings for the color overlay using an orange/yellow color:

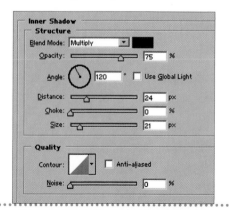

73. On the left-hand side select Inner Shadow. Enter the following settings for the inner shadow:

74. Select Inner Glow from the left-hand menu. Enter the following settings for the inner glow using an orange color:

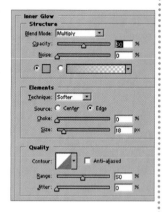

75. Select Bevel and Emboss from the left-hand menu. Enter the following settings for the bevel in the Layer Style dialog box using a blue shadow color:

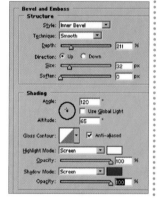

76. Select Contour from the left-hand menu. Change the contour to Half Round, check the Anti-aliased option, and leave the range at 50%.

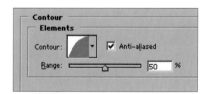

265

77. Select Pattern Overlay. Enter the following settings for the pattern overlay using an Optical Checkerboard pattern:

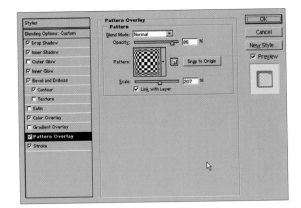

78. Lastly go to Stroke. Use the `PMW-project2-grad2.grd` gradient from the `project2.grd` gradient set on the CD. Enter the following stroke settings:

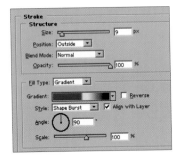

79. Click the New Style button to save the layer style. Name the new style. Once the style is saved, click OK to apply the style to the type.

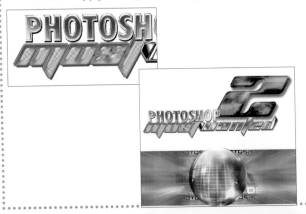

Ah, Al has applied his famous shiny metal and glass effect to the text. The only thing I see I want to change is the inside of the 'most' text. I will change the color to match the color on the "2".

80. Since Al was kind enough to keep the layer style intact, it will be really easy to change the color. Expand the layer styles on the text layer. Find the color overlay effect and double click it.

81. The Layer Style dialog box will open with the color overlay options shown. Click the color picker and change to a greenish color. Click OK.

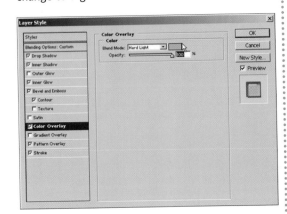

82. The change is now reflected on the text.

83. Let's open the Layer Style dialog box again and increase the drop shadow to make the text pop off the page:

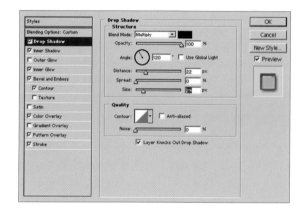

See the result:

84. We'll also apply a drop shadow to the rest of the text. Choose the text for most wanted and add a layer style. Here are the settings:

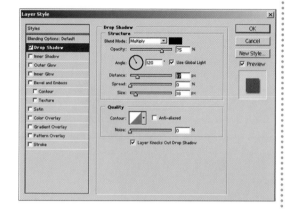

...and the result:

85. Before I pass it back to Al again, I think I'll add a burst of light behind the sphere to separate it from the background and also give it a bit of a 'wow' factor. Duplicate the sphere layer.

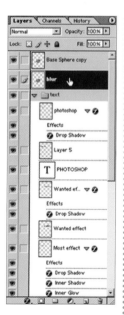

86. Add some noise to the blur layer by selecting Filter > Noise > Add Noise... Choose Gaussian for the distribution, as this gives a more random effect than uniform. Move the amount to the maximum.

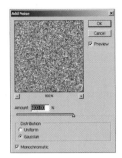

87. Now blur the globe layer with the noise added. The noise will help create streaks in the blur. Go to Filter > Blur > Radial Blur... Choose 100 and zoom for the method.

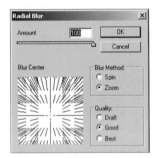

88. Duplicate the blurred layer several time to thicken it up:

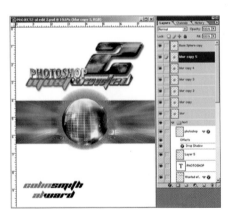

89. Merge all the blurred layers into one.

90. Apply the radial blur again twice. You'll see a good zoom effect beginning to be formed.

91. Duplicate the blurred layer again. Change the copied layer to Color Dodge mode.

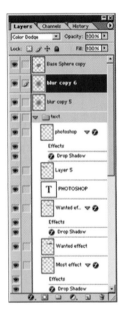

Make sure that the base sphere layer is under the blur layer for the effect to look correct. We now have a burst of light effect.

It looks like Colin has left it to me to work on the background a bit. Personally I like the cover now, but a little texture may help the cause.

92. To begin, open the image `RustyMetal.jpg` found on the CD.

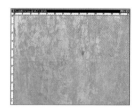

93. Hit CTRL/CMD+A to select the metal texture.

94. Hit CTRL/CMD+C to copy the rusty metal.

95. Return to the book cover image. Select the background layer and hit CTRL/CMD+V to paste the texture image into a new layer just above the background layer.

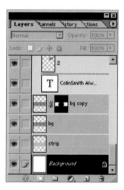

96. The resolutions between the two photos makes the pasted texture photo much smaller than the book cover. Go to Edit > Transform > Scale. Increase the size of the texture to cover the bottom portion of the book below the bar.

97. Duplicate the texture layer. Go to Edit > Transform > Flip Vertical. With the Move tool, place the new texture layer at the top of the book.

98. Again, go to Edit > Transform > Scale. Increase the height of the layer to cover the space between the bar and the top of the book cover image. Hit ENTER to accept the change.

99. Hit Ctrl/Cmd+E to merge the two texture layers together. Rename the newly merged layer 'Rust BG'.

100. Hit Ctrl/Cmd+Shift+L to apply Auto Levels to the texture layer.

101. As I work with this, Colin is offering his input and wants me to apply a blur. Let's see how it looks! Duplicate the Rust BG layer.

102. Go to Filter > Blur > Motion Blur... Enter the following blur settings and click OK:

103. Click the 'Create new fill or adjustment layer' icon, and select Hue/Saturation... from the menu. Enter the following settings in the 'Hue/Saturation' dialog box and click OK:

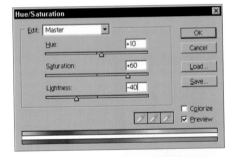

104. Hit CTRL/CMD+E twice to merge the Adjustment layer with the two texture layers.

105. One problem: now that the background has been darkened, the names are harder to read. CTRL/CMD-click the names layer.

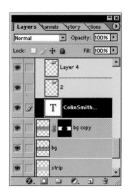

106. Create a new layer above the names layer.

107. Hit D and then X to place white in the foreground.

108. Go to Edit > Stroke... Enter the following Stroke settings using the white foreground color and click OK:

109. Hit CTRL/CMD+D to deselect.

110. Rename the stroke layer 'author outline'.

111. I'm not sure I like the way the texture goes straight to the edges of the book cover, so I'll try to dress those up a bit. Hit D to place black in the foreground color swatch.

112. Create a new layer above the Rust BG layer.

113. Select the Rectangular Marquee tool. In the Options bar, set the following attributes to the marquee:

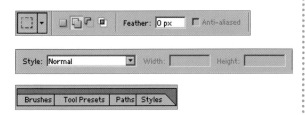

114. Make a selection over the bottom portion of the page, spanning from the bottom edge to above the names.

115. In the toolbox, select the Gradient tool. Set the following attributes for the Gradient tool in the Options bar using a foreground to transparent gradient:

116. Starting at the bottom of the page, draw the gradient up to a point just beyond the top selection border:

117. Hit CTRL/CMD+D to deselect.

118. Duplicate the gradient layer.

119. Go to Edit > Transform > Flip Vertical. Select the Move tool and place the new layer at the top of the page.

120. Let's make that center strip stand out a bit more. CTRL/CMD-click the strip layer to generate a selection.

121. Create a new layer above the 'author outline' layer.

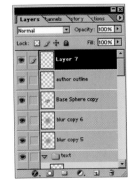

122. Go to Edit > Stroke... Enter the following stroke settings and click OK:

123. Hit CTRL/CMD+D to deselect.

124. CTRL/CMD-click the Sphere layer to generate a selection, but stay on the layer you just applied the stroke to. Hit the delete key to wipe away overlapping lines.

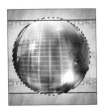

125. Hit CTRL/CMD+D to deselect.

126. Before I go, I'm not quite happy with the gradient blend I applied to the top and bottom of the page. Merge the two gradient layers, and select the newly merged layer. Select the Magic Wand tool and click in the open area between the gradients.

127. Go to Select > Inverse.

128. Go to Edit > Fill... Enter the following settings in the Fill dialog box and click OK:

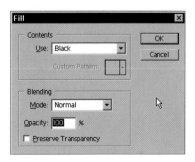

129. Hit CTRL/CMD+D to deselect. There...that border looks much better! I'm going to pass it to Colin now and let him tidy things up.

Looks like just a couple of things to look at and then we can wrap this one up.

130. The first thing I've done is added the 'effects and design tips' text.

131. Add a Drop Shadow to the new text.

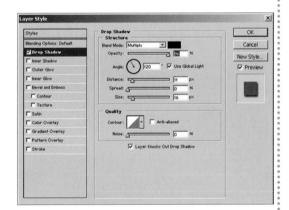

132. This helps lift it off the page.

273

133. We'll now create some shapes as a finishing touch. Create a new layer and name it 'shapes'.

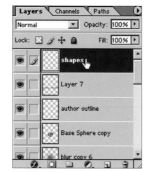

134. Choose the Polygon shape tool. Choose the settings shown here to create a hexagon. Make sure that Sides is set to 6.

135. Drag the tool on the page and release for the hexagon.

136. Drop the opacity to 34%.

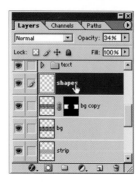

137. Here's what we have so far. We're going to add a solid white outline to the shape.

138. Load the selection from the hexagon.

139. Create a new layer above the hexagon layer.

140. Give the hexagon a 2 pixel stroke.

Here's our finished shape:

141. Merge the shape and shape stroke layers together.

142. Duplicate the hexagon several times and arrange on the page. Here's our final cover:

When designing for a client, it's standard practice to offer more than one idea for review. This design may be a bit 'busy' for some people's taste, so I removed the textures on the page and kept a cleaner black for the front. I also moved some of the shapes to balance the design a bit more. Once you're happy with the design you'll need to make a copy, merge all the layers and convert it to CMYK mode for printing. Save the file as a TIF or EPS file. You could either send it to the printers as an image file, or drop it into InDesign, Quark or Pagemaker for output.

Summary

I hope you've enjoyed these tutorials and learned a lot. I also hope you've had as much fun with these design projects as Al and I have in creating them. We wish you the best with your experimenting with the techniques you've learnt. Remember, be patient and keep practicing and you'll keep getting better as a designer. Some people are born with talent, but no one has produced excellent designs without practice. I'd also encourage you to visit www.photoshopcafe.com and www.actionfx.com regularly for more resources and ideas, and don't forget to drop by www.friendsofed.com to see a listing of the latest books available, take part in the forums, and read interviews with top designers. With a combination of good learning resources and practice, you're on the right road to producing some stunning designs!